THE ULTIMATE GUIDE TO CAMPING IN NATIONAL PARKS

59 ESSENTIALS FOR CAMPFIRE COOKING, BACKPACKING, FAMILY CAMPING, HIKING GEAR, AND EMERGENCY PLANNING

JAKE WARD

CONTENTS

INTRODUCTION

Work, Eat, Sleep; sometimes it feels like that is the sum of our lives. Life has become such a rush just trying to survive that we've forgotten how to live. So many of us are stressed; we don't find time to relax and eliminate all that stress. On the odd occasion that we do find a way to relax, we are held back by the limitations we place on ourselves. If you called up five friends and asked them to go camping, how many would say no simply because none of you know how to camp correctly?

Don't worry—you and your friends are not alone. Although camping is the perfect stress-relief activity because it allows you to physically and mentally distance yourself from the mundane responsibilities of life, many people shy away from it because they feel that they don't know enough to go camping.

In this guide, you will find everything about camping and the outdoors. You'll learn how to pick your campsite and what you need to be fully prepared. You'll even learn a few new skills to help you enjoy everything nature has to offer, and trust me; nature has a lot to offer you.

When you find yourself out in nature, you'll be disconnected from the modern world and, finally, be able to reconnect with yourself. You can reset and recharge whether you're highly active, love short trips, or want time to sit back and watch the flames dance.

Camping, however, can be about much more than finding yourself. The time you spend in nature and being more active than you usually would than sitting behind a desk all day have some impressive health benefits. Soon, you will enjoy your life a whole lot more.

Now, at this point, you're probably starting to wonder who this person is who's trying to get you to run off into the woods. Allow me to introduce myself; as the book's cover may have given away, my name is Jake Ward. Throughout my entire life, I've found myself almost fascinated with nature. All I wanted to do was be outside, where I could see the plants and trees create unique and beautiful patterns with their branches and leaves, hear the crickets chirp the night away, and the birds sing the day into play. This passion of mine led me to start camping as soon as I could express that desire to my parents, and it continues to keep me doing so.

During these wonderful years of camping in as many different environments as I could get myself into, I've gained extensive knowledge and way too many skills. Not that you'll hear me complaining, however! However, on the topic of camping skills, I noted another aspect, which is the biggest drive in wanting to share this knowledge I accumulated.

I've seen so many people cut their break short simply because when they finally got to the campsite, they realized there was some knowledge they lacked, and instead of learning it, they packed up and left. These people included families with an array of children, fathers, and sons on bonding trips, young couples looking for some alone time, and even some single souls who needed a personal adventure.

Whenever I saw the defeated look on someone's face as they rolled up their sleeping bags and carefully organized their car, I wished to share all my knowledge with them so they could enjoy nature as much as I did. Unfortunately, most people, especially inexperienced campers, don't take kindly to total strangers approaching them in a remote area.

Instead, I decided to write this guide you can always carry with you, filled with everything you need to know to have a safe, affordable, enjoyable, and environmentally sustainable break from the world.

1

CAMPING IN NATIONAL PARKS

N1ational parks are the best place to find safe, legal, and appealing camping sites. Luckily, regardless of what country you find yourself in, I can guarantee that your country will have an abundance of national parks to choose from. So, let's take a closer look at camping and what camping in national parks entails.

WHAT TO EXPECT WHEN CAMPING IN A NATIONAL PARK

When you go camping in a national park, you will have many choices for how you can camp. You will have options from as minimalistic as possible, where you only use a sleeping bag and a few other minor tools, to full-on tent camping and to luxurious camping, where you enjoy an RV with running water and electricity.

Regardless of your camping style, a few expectations will remain the same. You will, of course, experience the absolute beauty of nature first and foremost. Each national park will boast its array of unique flora and fauna. For example, the Saguaro National Park boasts of being one of the few places where you can see the Saguaro cactus in its natural habitat as well as the unique inhabitants of the Sonoran Desert.

On the other hand, the Kruger National Park in South Africa boasts about their wildlife, including the famous "Big Five," a large assortment of other African wildlife, and some of its unique bushveld flora.

Depending on which national park you decide to visit, you might get to camp and move between wildlife and flora that might be less protected. One thing, however, is sure: you will always experience something unique at each national park you visit.

When you spend the night in a protected ecosystem with everything it offers, you will have a fantastic time seeing the stars, the world around you, and even yourself for a change. The key to truly enjoying this spectacular experience is to prepare yourself.

#1—A PLAN

Now that we know what to expect, we can look at the first of our 59 essentials. This would be your plan. There is a saying that goes, "Failing to plan is planning to fail." This cannot be truer. Before embarking on an adventure, you must know your adventure to ensure you are well prepared.

It would be best to decide where to go to formulate the best plan for your adventure. Do you want to visit a park close to you? Or do you want to see a park somewhere entirely new for you? For beginners, stay closer to home. Aside from making travel more manageable, you know weather patterns in your area better than in a new country; this can be very important for a new camper.

Once you have decided where to go, you must choose when you want to go. Most of us can only take some time away from work and life each year. In addition, we often don't have much control over when we take off, as we need to consider how busy work will be, when others are taking off, and even when we will have built up enough leave days. As if that doesn't make taking a trip hard enough, most parks will suggest that you visit at certain times of the year to enjoy the natural beauty to the fullest. Some even refuse entry or extended stay when natural conditions may make the park dangerous. So, be sure you know when you can go, which might mean that you need to book well in advance.

Although your circumstances only allow you to plan so far in advance, it is always good to plan as far ahead as possible, even when unnecessary. Most parks work on a first-come, first-served system, which means that if you don't book in time, there won't be a place for you. Remember that the park recommends the safest and most appealing time of the year to everyone, so depending on the popularity of your chosen destination, you may need to book up to a year in advance to get a good spot during the best times.

Please also look at the activities available within your chosen national park. Since the primary purpose of most parks is to ensure the protection and continued survival of their ecosystems, some activities like fishing or rock climbing might be banned to protect particular flora and fauna from extinction or prevent the entire ecosystem from collapsing. Most parks will still have designated areas for you to fulfill a variety of activities. So, you will need to see what activities are allowed to plan your days and what you must bring along.

You will also need to consider what you can bring into the park. Most parks do not allow alcohol for safety, but other aspects, such as certain size vehicles not being allowed, make camping with an RV or trailer impossible. In general, looking at the rules of a park is a must.

Next, Let's look into the costs connected to the adventure. While almost every park offers a season pass, you may still need to pay separately for access to camping grounds and even some activities in the park. This means you must make a budget and be sure you can afford the trip. As an added tip, remember to add your travel fees to your budget early on.

Lastly, investigate what animals live in the park. Some animals, like bears, tend to enter camps looking for food, so knowing what animals you encounter will help you see what extra precautions to take.

We'll look more into some of these aspects early on, and they are all important to creating the first and largest essential of your adventure: a plan. The most critical elements of your plan are knowing when you are going, where you will be going, what you will be doing, and how you will do it.

#2—RULES AND REGULATIONS

In the previous section, I mentioned looking at the rules and regulations while planning your trip. Yes, that is important, but it is also important to print out the rules of wherever you are camping and keep them with you.

This might sound ridiculous and overly careful. Still, since every park has different creatures and plants that thrive within its confines, its rules and regulations often include unique points for interacting with these plants and animals. This is why it's crucial to have a set of rules and regulations to refer to when you need clarification.

Some rules are common to all parks, so to help you understand what to expect better, here is a list of the most common rules you will find.

What You Bring In, You Must Take Out Again

Due to the sensitive nature of ecosystems and their protected statuses, you must ensure you leave as little behind as possible. When you leave, take all your equipment and belongings with you. While in the park, take a small bag with you everywhere you go, and if you put it down, secure it so it cannot blow away. This bag is for anything you need to discard, whether it is food packaging or a piece of the food itself. You can also always add any trash you might come across—this way, you can help improve the park and minimize the impact on other visitors.

This bag should be discarded in trash bins and areas designated by the park. If you cannot find any, keep it with you until you leave and dump it in the closest bin outside the park.

Don't Feed the Animals

You may think it's cute when an animal walks up to you when you have something in your hand, and you may believe this animal wants your food or drink. Regardless of whether this is true, please do not feed the animals your food unless the park rules specifically state that it is okay. While most foods are ok for animals to consume, most human foods are highly processed and changed, and some things in our food can cause harm to these animals. When wildlife gets sick, it can easily upset the park's ecosystem, and repairing that damage or just healing one sick animal can cost a lot of money. That's why it's best to keep your food to yourself.

Don't Pick Flowers

Like animals, flowers exist in a delicate balance, and many of the flora in also protected species. Simply picking a flower or taking a sprout from a plant could end up causing irreparable damage to the plant and its ecosystem. Most parks will have strict rules against interacting with plant life in any way.

Firewood

You may see wood as just another piece of equipment that has no impact on anything, but this is not necessarily true. Firewood can and usually does contain certain insects that, if left unchecked, could cause harm to other plant life. Many of these insects are native to only certain types of wood but can spread to other plants and trees when you burn the firewood. To get firewood, avoid damaging any trees or plants in the park. Instead, most parks will have firewood available for purchase or allow you to pick up dead branches from the ground. You should also never leave with any wood from a park because you never know what else you might be carrying out with you.

Fire

When camping, it is only natural to start a fire. Whether the goal is to keep yourself warm at night or to cook your food, a fire is necessary. Unfortunately, as much as we rely on fire to exist, it can be destructive. Therefore, all parks have strict rules regarding fires. These rules vary from having a fire in designated areas to only allowing fires under certain conditions. You must always check whether a fire is allowed before creating one. Even if a fire is permitted, you must be cautious to ensure it does not spread out of control. This can be achieved by creating a fire pit, only making small or preferably no fires during intense winds, and killing the fire and embers entirely before leaving the area or going to sleep.

Swimming

Nothing is better than jumping into cool water on a hot day, and the bodies of water in national parks can seem inviting, especially if it's a spring or a pool beneath a waterfall. The problem is that you cannot know how your presence will impact the creatures and plants dependent on these water bodies. Even stepping a foot beneath the surface of the water could cause destruction. The general rule of thumb here is to not swim in any area not marked as safe.

Caves

If you want to go camping, it usually means you are adventurous, and adventurous people love exploring. So, when you find a cave, your curiosity will tempt you to switch on your flashlight and look inside. Although it's natural to want to do so, it's best that you don't. Most caves are habitats for various creatures, from bats to bears, snakes, scorpions, and much more. Entering the cave can cause many creatures that call it home to flee and avoid it in the future, causing an upset in the ecosystem. Aside from that, caves are extremely dangerous, and if you get injured, it's even more challenging to find you inside a cave.

Artifacts

Many national parks are built to protect the eco, ancient cultures, and their legacies. It's not unheard of for campers, hikers, and even tourists to stumble across some artifacts with archeological significance. If you are lucky enough to do so, don't touch anything. Take a picture, retrace your steps carefully, and inform the park officials as quickly as possible. The park will then call in the correct people for the job.

Vehicles and Drones

Let's start with vehicles. Vehicles are only to be driven on approved routes. This includes your car, dirt bikes, and ATVs. Your car will usually only be allowed to travel on predetermined roads between the park entrance, facilities, and your camping site. Dirt bikes and ATVs are sometimes allowed on specific trails, but because that is not common, check whether the park allows them before you bring them along.

On the other hand, drones usually are entirely banned in national parks. Unfortunately, although our technology has improved quite a lot, these devices can still easily be blown off course by strong winds and cause distress among the animals in the park. Some animals may even believe the drone to be another creature or its prey and attempt to attack it, hurting itself. If you have a drone that you wish to fly, you will generally need to get written permission from the park authorities well in advance.

Pets

Regarding pets, especially dogs, we see them as a part of the family. This means we usually want to take them with us on our adventures. When possible, however, please don't take your pets with you. They are still animals and have animal instincts, so they might try to hunt the native animals or fall prey to one. If you take your pets with you and the park allows them in, ensure you do not let them off-leash unless they are locked in your tent or RV with you. Also, make sure to pick up their feces and cover their urine. You should also try your best to ensure that they do their business only around your campground, as most animals in the park rely on scents to identify dangers and territories. When your pet adds its scent to the ecosystem, it can cause confusion and damage.

#3—PASSPORTS

It might sound ridiculous to carry your passport with you everywhere. But remember that your passport is a form of identification, and the one thing we place above everything else is safety. Sometimes, safety means carrying identification with you. Aside from that, many parks will need to see some identification when you claim your reservation, and when you always have your passport ready and valid, the world and all its national parks are at your fingertips.

#4—ITINERARY

We'll broach safety again with this essential. Having that plan out what activities you're doing each day helps you with your planning and packing and can be used by others to look for you if you are injured or lost. Your itinerary can speed up any potential rescue and ensure your safety. Of course, as I mentioned, an itinerary also helps you make the most out of your adventure. Please don't see it as a strict schedule but as a reminder of all the fun activities you can enjoy. We can become so engrossed in relaxing that we forget we can also do something fun!

#5—TICKETS/ANNUAL PASSES

You must book in advance to get into most national parks, especially camping. This means you will most likely have a ticket connected to your camping site that you will need to present to the park officials upon entry. Many countries also offer annual passes that allow entrance to multiple parks without having to buy tickets every time. It will still mean you must reserve your camping site and pay a small fee for the campsite. For beginner campers, see if your country offers annual passes that allow entry to several national parks. This can make your camping trip much cheaper and motivate you to enjoy these parks' beauty.

Most countries offer a variety of annual passes with discounts based on age, whether you're a student or even military background. These passes are usually valid for one or two people and allow free entry with a vehicle to all connected parks. Since the state owns most parks, this means that you will have access to the majority of parks in your country. While these passes allow free entry, they also usually allow free entry for one vehicle and, in some countries, all vehicle occupants. So, purchasing an annual pass may be the key to turning your solo adventures into a great date or even a fun family outing.

#6—PERMITS AND LICENSES

National parks offer various activities, from dirt bikes to fishing, rock climbing, and many more. However, almost all these activities require a license or permit to engage in them, and you should tell the national park you have been trained to do it safely. I suggest having a folder with all your licenses and permits—that way, if you decide on a new activity you may not have realized is available, you can do so without a problem. At the very least, you should always have the license and permits for the activities you plan to engage in. The national park website will usually hold the answer if you are unsure whether a specific activity requires a license or permit.

SO, WHAT DO WE KNOW?

Your camping trip will be a breeze if you always have these first six essentials ready. Well, that's at least until you get to the campsite, but we'll get there in a moment.

It would be best if you were well-prepared to plan your trip, get to your campsite, have all your documentation ready, and know what activities you can and will engage in versus what is against the rules. In the next chapter, we will examine how the different seasons impact your trip and how to prepare for them.

2

MUST-KNOWS BEFORE HEADING TO YOUR CAMPING ADVENTURE

As I've already mentioned, each national park will have specific times of the year when it is the ideal time to visit. Although most of these parks will suggest visiting during spring or summer, specific events and animals often can better be observed during other times of the year. This means you must know how to prepare for each season. You also have the matter of camping with your family without a vehicle. In this chapter, we will investigate all these different aspects of camping and learn how to prepare for them.

SPRING

Since this will be one of the most suggested times of the year to visit a national park, it is only fitting that we start with spring. Spring is an exciting time in the wilderness. Most animals give birth during this time, and most plants will bloom and start to bear fruit. It can be a beautiful and magical time, but spring comes with its own set of challenges.

Weather

The first challenge we will investigate is the weather. During springtime, we have the last angry attempts of winter to keep the world in its clutches, while at the same time, summer fights for its turn. Because of this, the weather can turn suddenly from one extreme to the other, often bringing rain-fall with it.

Before you head out on your camping adventure, check the weather forecast for the period you will be camping and be prepared for both warm and cold weather. Taking along umbrellas and raincoats is always a good idea during spring-time, as you can never be sure when a storm might form. On your trip, make sure that you take cover and get back to your campgrounds as soon as the weather looks like it might turn to rain. You don't want to be caught in the open unless you know the terrain well.

Clothing

When you pack your clothing, remember how low temper-atures can reach in the spring, especially if you are camping in a desert or relatively flat and open places. Considering this, pack enough clothing that can be worn in layers. This helps keep you warm when the temperature drops. Still, it allows you to transition to more excellent clothing when the temperature warms up again, so you won't overheat and dehydrate quickly. Remember always to have waterproof clothing for those unexpected spring showers.

Hydration and Staying Dry

Taking enough drinking water with you is essential because the weather can switch quickly from warm and dry to wet and cold. One of the biggest dangers we face when camping is dehydration, especially if you are the adventurous type that likes to do other activities like hiking and rock climbing. While the morning temperature might look cool and breezy, the afternoon sun could quickly turn brutally hot, so always take more water than you think you need.

While water inside your body is critical, water outside is a no-go. To help you stay dry and protected even during the most intense rain showers, get a tarp that fits over your tent and some rain boots to keep your feet dry and mud-free.

Bugs

As the animals start to breed and give birth to their young, so do the insects. Although they might take longer to emerge from their winter hideaways, their lifespans are shorter, so they will pop up in swarms almost overnight. Mosquitoes, flies, gnats, and many other pests will soon await you. So, don't forget to look at bug sprays, mosquito nets, and other protection against these terrors.

Animals

I've mentioned it several times, but we must give animals their section here. When spring comes along, animals hibernating all winter start to wake up. While this is a beautiful piece of the natural cycle, it also means these animals are hungry and will be foraging for food. It's not uncommon for some of these animals to wander into campgrounds when they smell the delicious meal you will undoubtedly be cooking for yourself. Luckily, you don't need to worry too much as most animals have learned to stay away from humans, but you must still be vigilant. When researching the park for your trip, please pay special attention to the animals and forewarnings of animals known to invite themselves to your dinner table. Also, keep your food packed and secured whenever you leave your campsite.

SUMMER

As the seasons move on, nature can change quite a bit. Luckily, since summertime is the time that most people go camping, it's also the season that is both the easiest to prepare for and the one that most people are already prepared for. When you see people camping on television or hear camp stories, most of it is during the summer. The weather is a bit more stable, and you don't have to worry too much about sudden showers putting you in danger. At the same time, you can observe almost all the animals and plants while they thrive and enjoy lazy days before the hustle of getting ready for winter starts again. If you go camping during the summer, ensure your adventure is planned and booked well in advance since this is the most popular time of the year. You might also want to stock up on camping supplies over the winter when the shops are less busy.

Weather

Summer brings the heat. In some areas, this heat can be scorching and dangerous. So, aside from your hydration, which we will look at in a moment, ensure you have a hat, lots of sunscreen, and any other protection you can find from that flaming ball in the sky. Limit your time in the sun and plan your activities so that you have more than enough time to rest and recover. Sunstroke and dehydration are just as dangerous as hypothermia or an injury. Too much time in the scorching heat can cause you to become delirious, which could lead to injuries. This is why you must also ensure that your activities are done in areas with much shade where you can rest.

Clothing

While we all automatically receive forewarnings and more relaxed clothing during summertime, remember that this leaves large pieces of our bodies exposed to the sun and the critters of the wild. The best option is to find breathable clothing that keeps you cool and protects your skin from the sun, insects, and other animals that might want to taste your exposed skin. Just ensure that you never overdress and cause your body to overheat; as I've already mentioned, heat can be just as dangerous as cold.

Hydration

This is the most critical time of the year to keep yourself hydrated. A general rule in the backpacking community is to have one liter of water, or roughly 34 fluid ounces, for every hour of hiking. I suggest doubling this amount. Each person should have about two liters of water, or about 55 fluid ounces, per hour away from your campsite.

Before leaving your campsite for any adventure, you should also find a map of watering spots where you will be hiking, climbing, or doing any other activity. That way, if you start running low on water, you can refill at a watering hole before you run out.

Water is the most critical aspect of a summer advance that should be remembered. Also, ensure that you and anyone joining you consume enough water throughout the day, even if you stay at the camping site. Always keep an eye out for signs of dehydration, and make sure to get medical assistance immediately if you think someone is not looking well.

Bugs

While spring sees the critters start to come out, they will never be as abundant as they are during summer. The heat and increased animal activity will create fertile feeding and breeding grounds for these pests. Before you know it, they will be everywhere you look in more fantastic varieties and numbers than before. Fortunately, spring has prepared you for this, so you should have bug sprays, zappers, nets, and anything else you can think of. Remember to check if your destination has diseases that mosquito bites, such as malaria, can spread, so you can adequately prepare before going on your adventure.

Animals

The summer means leisure time in the animal kingdom. During springtime, most animals quench their big hunger after the winter. The steps necessary for population growth have been thoroughly enjoyed, and most animals have already given birth to their offspring or are close to doing so. This means that animals will only hunt and scavenge for food when needed and spend most of their time conserving energy, looking after their young, and enjoying the summer sun. This makes summer a perfect time for adventures, including a safari or something similar. Still, it also means your chances of encountering an animal lounging around during your activities are greater. Enjoy this but stay vigilant and don't trespass where animals hunt or keep their young.

FALL

As the seasons progress, we move from the warm, lazy days of summer to the shorter and colder days of fall. As the trees shed their leaves and prepare for their slumber, some animals stockpile food for the winter, others prepare themselves for a long sleep, and many engage in mating rituals so that their young are born in the warmer months when food is abundant. Looking at this, you can see another beautiful side to nature. Although I suggest a fall camping trip at least once to see this beauty, fall brings new challenges.

Weather

After the summer equinox, the days progressively get shorter. This means you might not fit in the same number of activities you normally would while on your adventure, but it does give you a better opportunity to observe the national park's nocturnal life. Remember that you'll experience similar weather challenges with spring, but this time, depending on where you are in the world, you'll also face the chance of snowfall. If you camp in the fall, I suggest you go early when the weather is still lovely. However, don't forget to check your weather report and pack for extreme cold and warm weather.

Clothing

As mentioned in the previous section, it ranges from nice and sunny to icy cold. So, take layered clothing, thermal underwear, and any other temperature-resistant clothing you can find. Don't overdress on warm days; have something warm you can put on if the weather changes. It's a good idea to check the weather forecast before starting any activity. Since most national parks have poor reception, you will probably need to do this before leaving your campsite.

Hydration

As the weather starts to cool, you will need less hydration than during the summer months. Don't let this fool you, though; just because it is cooler does not mean you should carry less water with you, as you might not realize how thirsty you are. You never know if you need to hydrate extra or if a watering spot is out of order.

Bugs

As animals start hiding away, bugs and insects will do the same. You will see fewer flies and mosquitoes, especially on colder days. However, that does not mean they will be nonexistent. Pack your bug spray and keep as much skin covered as you can without overheating.

Animals

During the fall, the creatures hibernating during winter eat more to build up fat reserves. This means they might be busier than usual but will be gone from sight very soon. So, any sighting currently is rare and wonderful!

WINTER

And finally, we reach the coldest season. Like most of us who want to stay in bed under blankets with a warm cup of coffee when it gets cold outside, most animals do the same. That doesn't mean there's no adventure to be found, however. Many animals, like squirrels and deer, thrive during the winter months. There are even some bear species that remain active during the winter. Another positive of winter is that this is usually seen as an off-season with fewer people and more nature.

Weather

When the cold kicks in, the dangers of hypothermia and frostbite skyrocket. During the winter months, take every precaution to keep the heat in and the cold out. This can be done by laying tarps under and over your tent, putting sleeping foam under your sleeping bag, and bringing a whole array of equipment that we'll investigate further in the next chapter. The cold is the biggest challenge you will face when camping in the winter.

Clothing

With the freezing temperatures set in, you should wear as many layers of clothing as you can to keep you warm, from thermal underwear to proper gloves, scarves, and headwear. Don't forget to look at warmer socks and shoes as well—we often forget that we need to protect our feet just as much as the rest of our bodies. Waterproof shoes are necessary during winter because your feet may get wet in snow and water.

Bugs

Another good thing about winter is that bugs are almost nonexistent. The usual suspects, like flies and mosquitoes, are gone, but ants, termites, spiders, and beetles can still be abundant. So, make sure that you protect yourself from these little critters.

Animals

As I've mentioned, although many animals hibernate and prefer to stay in their winter habitats, others can be found out and about. During winter, it might also be best to camp closer to the poles since this might be the perfect time to observe cold-weather animals like polar bears. Wherever you choose to camp, check the park's website to see what animals are active during winter.

CAMPING WITH KIDS

Camping can be a fun family activity. But, when you add children, you add a lot more responsibility to your camping trip. Of course, kids are not the easiest to convince about camping fun, especially with the need for more signal and electricity. Because of this, many people shy away from introducing kids to a camping lifestyle. I want to reassure you that camping with kids isn't impossible. The key is introducing them to camping correctly, ensuring they are well-prepared, and finding new and exciting ways to stimulate them on camping trips. After all, a camping trip probably is not that different from the games they play.

Introducing Your Kids to Camping

The first step is to introduce your kids to camping in a way that excites them to join you on this adventure. One way to do this is through reverse psychology, especially if they are older. Go on a few camping trips yourself and take many pictures! When you return, don't hesitate to tell your kids how much fun you had, what activities you did, or even what animals you saw. Create interest for your kids and let them accompany you on your next trip. They will often be more inclined to do so if they think it's their idea.

Of course, there is no better time to start camping with your kids than when they are still young. If your toddlers grow up exposed to camping, it will make camping trips much more effortless. When camping with toddlers, however, you will want to look at national parks closer to home that offer more everyday activities, like short and level hikes near clear streams where you don't have to worry about staying balanced or stopping your toddler from running around the entire time. As they grow up, you can look at more adventurous sites and activities that will keep them stimulated. But we'll investigate this in a moment.

If your kids are a bit older but not yet teenagers, a great way to prepare them for camping is backyard camping with lots of fun activities like making s'mores on the fire, looking at the stars, and telling campfire stories. This will give your kids a sense of what camping is about, and you can always add stories of your camping adventures to get them more excited about the real deal.

Teenagers are a bit more complicated. They already know everything and don't want to spend time trapped in the woods with no signal and only their family for conversation. So, take a more adult approach with them by including them in your planning and allowing them to help choose the national park and even work out your itinerary if they feel like they have a voice instead of being dragged along.

Preparing Your Kids

Once you've introduced your kids to camping and excited them enough to join you, you must prepare them. By appropriately preparing your kids before a camping trip, you ensure that they are safety conscious from the start, and you can even make sure that the parts they might see as boring, such as setting up camp, are completed faster and more efficiently.

One of the best ways to prepare your kids for the real thing is to do a few dry runs before you go. With younger kids, the background camping idea is an excellent time to have them leather to prepare and introduce them to the idea of camping. Please ensure they are around when you stand in the backyard, and even ask them to help you with small tasks such as handing you a tent pin or holding onto the tarp. When you finally get to the campsite, you can remind your young kids how you did it in the backyard so they stay close while you set up.

For older kids, you could always ask for help. As discussed in the next chapter, checking your equipment before your trip, including setting up your tent, is essential. You can always ask your kids to help you check that the equipment is still in good condition; that way, you give them responsibility and show that you trust their judgment. While helping check the equipment, they will undoubtedly learn how to set up your camp. This means that when you arrive on your camping trip, they will already be prepared to help you set up.

Of course, there is more to camping than setting up the camp. You will also need to prepare your kids for the activities you plan on doing. This can be done by taking them on a walk through your neighborhood for roughly the same distance as a hike you might be planning. Remember to take your time and go easy. By finding more accessible versions of the activities you are planning, you will prepare your kids for the activities themselves. For example, if you take a walk through your neighborhood and your kids run out of water, not only do you know to pack extra water for them on the hike, but they will have learned to conserve their water when you go on the actual hike.

Another aspect of preparing your kids for camping is letting them prepare themselves. Instead of packing their bags for them, allow them to pack them. You can give them an essential checklist of what they will need and always recheck their bags before leaving. This way, you not only teach them responsibility and how to look after themselves, but you also give them the choice of what they want to wear and take along. If your kids don't like the fact that you recheck their bags before leaving, you can always make an extra bag with the basics they will need and sneak it into the car. You don't need to tell them about it unless they forget something.

Making It Stress-Free and Fun

Okay, so you introduce your kids to the idea of camping, prepare them for it, and finally get them there; now what? The first thing you need to do is to breathe. The parents are often the most significant factor during a camping trip. But don't worry, that's a good thing.

My first tip is to get to the campsite as early as possible, so you have enough light to set up your camp. As much as you prepared yourself and your kids for setting up, it will undoubtedly take longer with them there. Aside from that, it's easier to get them to help you with something they don't want to do while they still have lots of energy, as opposed to when they are tired.

You want to keep a positive and happy mood during the trip. When kids are out in nature, their reactions are difficult to predict. Some may be so excited that they easily get distracted, and others may be so unimpressed that they are in a bad mood the entire time. The key to getting them to enjoy themselves and want to return is not becoming unhappy with their reactions. So, don't get impatient when you are trying to set up the tent as soon as you arrive and they seem distracted or more interested in something else, don't get impatient. Instead, try indulging them for a moment; if you see they are distracted by the nearby trees, offer a quick hike so they can see the area before you put up the tent.

This flexibility will allow them to enjoy the trip themselves, engage their curiosity, and make them feel like they are on an adventure instead of just trotting along on their adventure. You will need to remain flexible during the entire trip.

They might discover a new activity that interests them or realize they are not interested in one of the activities you already have planned. When you show them flexibility, they will be more prone to showing you flexibility.

Of course, most of your time will be spent at the camping ground, so you must find a way to keep your kids happy and entertained there. Younger kids are easier to entertain, and the addition of battery-powered fairy lights, glowsticks, marshmallows, and other tasty and shiny things will keep them busy. Teenagers are a bit more complicated. They often prefer playing d spending time on their electronics. Most important, however, is their own space. If you have a teenager camping with you, consider setting up a separate tent for them. Remember that in your teenage years, you are often uncomfortable in your skin, especially as your body changes. This means that sharing a small, confined space with your family is sometimes nothing less than absolute hell. The first tip is to have their tent. You are adding to their comfort and enjoyment.

Of course, there is one aspect of camping that everyone needs to accept and get used to quickly, especially someone camping with younger kids. Yes, the dirt, mud, sticks, leaves, and anything else the kids will probably pick up, play in, and get stuck in. In the next chapter, I'll mention some essentials to combat the amount of dirt you will inevitably be exposed to, but it's best to accept early on that you will get dirtier with kids joining your trip.

Lastly, one of the easiest ways to ensure the kids enjoy a camping trip is by having some of their favorite foods and treats available. When you are home, your kids are used to having a routine and responsibilities, just like you do. They also need to finish homework, study for tests, eat at a specific time, and go to bed at a specific time. A camping trip is also a chance for them to escape the world momentarily. So, let them indulge in some of their favorite things. Of course, I'm not saying to forget any form of nutrition completely, but since they will be more active, they can afford to enjoy their guilty pleasures more. So, plan to have one of their favorite meals for every or three days you are on the trip. This is guaranteed to shine a happy light on their memories of the trip.

CAMPING WITHOUT A CAR

Before heading to the bulk of our 59 essentials, I want to share a different camping method with you. Try this method until you are experienced in camping. With this method, you have limited supplies and equipment and need help to get more easily. This can also be a more expensive camping choice than packing your car with everything you need.

This method will include only taking what you can physically carry to go camping and using public transport. While it is a lot more challenging, it can be the perfect answer for someone who wants to take a solo journey. Although this journey can be independent and freeing, I want to stress the importance of planning it out before leaving on your journey and making sure someone knows exactly what your plan is, where you are headed, and when you should be expected back. There is nothing more important than safety.

How to Camp Without a Car

Since this is a unique and challenging way of camping, I'll share step-by-step instructions to make this much more manageable.

Step 1: Choose Your Destination

The first step is knowing where you want to go. Since you will rely on public transport and carry all your equipment on your back, you must carefully consider your preferred camping ground. Make sure it is accessible using public transport or walk there with all your belongings from the nearest public transport.

Step 2: Planning

As we already know, your plan is an essential aspect of your adventure. This will determine what you need to take along. So, plan all your activities while keeping your limited space and travel capacity in mind. Also, find out if you can have supplies delivered to your camping site. There are several great businesses accessed through apps on your smartphone that can bring you food and other essentials, which will mean that you wouldn't have to carry all that with you. However, some parks will not allow deliveries, so determine whether this is allowed. Some parks might even stop you from receiving the deliveries at their gate and carrying them in, depending on how strict their rules are.

Step 3: Packing

Everything you need must fit into your backpack and one or two more handbags. To this end, investigate getting camping gear that is lightweight and compact, such as lightweight tents. Be careful of inflatable equipment as it tends to be as heavy as it is compact. Paper plates are lightweight and easier to pack away, and your water bottle can be used to drink almost anything. Do what you can to minimize what you bring, but make sure you don't compromise on safety. It's also an excellent idea to evenly distribute the weight in your bags, making it easier to carry.

Step 4: Traveling

Before leaving for your trip, make sure your routes are planned out and memorized. You need to know where you can take public transport and where you have to walk. The authors have made this more manageable since you probably have some map and GPS navigation on your phone. When you are confident of your route, please purchase your tickets, such as bus and train tickets, in advance, and keep them in a safe but easily accessible place. This makes it easier to get onto your public transport. Also, give yourself enough time to get to your transport and don't buy tickets requiring you to rush at timeslots. Don't forget to plan rest stops where you can take a breather, eat something, and rehydrate appropriately before starting your journey.

Step 5: Arrive and Enjoy

Assuming everything works out, you will be at your camping site, or at least within walking distance of your camping site, within no time. Once you've arrived, make sure you set up your camp as quickly as possible so that you have space to relax and you can quite literally take a load off your shoulders. Don't forget to enjoy the destination; it is, after all, the goal of your journey.

Step 6: Leave

The hardest step in this adventure is packing up and facing the real world again. While you are packing, take extra care to leave as little of yourself behind as possible so that we can preserve the parks for the next person to enjoy. Ensure all your waste is disposed of correctly and you have all your belongings. Your bags should also be lighter on the journey back as your consumables should be used up, and since you already know how to get between your home and the park, the journey should be much easier and simpler for you.

Tips

- Most national parks and campsites have shuttles that travel between nearby airports and train stations, which can make your journey easier.
- If your destination doesn't allow deliveries, you can always schedule a delivery at your last stop before heading into the park. This might be heavier, but you won't have to carry those items from home.
- If you make a no-car camping trip during spring or fall, you can wear more clothes to free up packing space.
- Most national parks offer firewood or charcoal, so you don't have to carry that.
- Most national parks also have built-in barbecue facilities or allow you to bring in a disposable barbecue, which is lightweight and makes your return journey easier.
- If camping during warm and dry summer months, you can forgo a tent and sleep under the stars. Alternatively, some parks offer camping or even glamping facilities.
- Most of your equipment and essentials can cater to two people, so making this journey with a friend or

partner does not necessarily mean you need to bring more things aside from their personal effects.

SO, WHAT DO WE KNOW?

Camping can be done in any season, but it will always require lots of planning and preparation. Each season comes with its list of pros and cons, along with its challenges and rewards. Regardless of when you go on your adventure, it will be the break you want and bring the enjoyment you deserve.

Whether camping with your kids, being flexible outside of your routine, taking a more significant break from everything, or adventuring only with the things you can carry, there will always be certain things that are not optional for your camping trip. In the next chapter, we will investigate the basics of shelter. This includes everything from your shelter to what you will sleep in and how to wash the adventure off yourself every night before bed.

3

CAMPING SHELTERS, SLEEPING KITS, AND HYGIENE

We'll finally get into the bulk of our 59 essentials for camping. First, we'll ensure you have a safe and warm resting place while camping. Then, we'll ensure your fellow campers don't mistake you for Bigfoot!

#7—TENTS

Although it is possible to go camping in a tent, I recommend something other than that for beginners. Although tents may sound simple, they it more complicated than you think. The first time I went camping, I thought all I had to do was go out and buy a small one-person tent, and that would be it. Boy, was I mistaken! Let's look at the differences available, their pros and cons, and when they will be the most fitting.

Dome Tents

These tents have become extremely popular in recent years thanks to their easy set-up and incredible versatility. If you are starting your camping journey and don't have a preferred region or season yet, this is the tent to look at. These tents only have two poles placed across each other and inserted into the "floor" of the tent. This way, it creates a dome-shaped structure that keeps itself up.

Pros

- The shape and size of the tent allow wind, rain, and other debris to effortlessly move around it and fall to the ground, making it well-suited for all weather conditions.
- Set-up is quick and can be done quickly by a single person.
- They usually have waterproof flooring.
- A dome tent can be single-layered or double-layered, meaning that in the summer, it can be a cool refuge that keeps the bugs and heat out, while during other months, the second layer can help protect you from rain and snow to some extent, the cold.

Cons

- The tents are usually small, and the walls and ceiling are lower than others due to their shape.
- Powerful winds can flatten it because it only has two poles.
- Some dome tents come in only a single layer, sacrificing breathability.
- They have little adaptability to offer extra space or shade, even outside.

A-Frame Tents

These are the traditional tents we are accustomed to seeing in movies. They were the most popular tents for the longest time due to their simple designs. These tents are usually supported by only two poles in the middle and an m between them, giving their "A" shape. The simplistic design gave this tent popularity, but some inherent flaws led to its downfall. This design has, however, remained popular for lightweight camping.

Pros

- These tents can be extremely lightweight and compact.
- The poles can serve a dual purpose.

Cons

- The structure of this design is weak and flimsy, leaving it vulnerable to strong winds.
- The sloped sides of these tents often allow water and mud to collect.
- They can be challenging to set up alone.
- Each tent only has a small and confined space.
- They usually don't have excellent ventilation or breathability.

Cabin Tents

These are larger and resemble a cabin or house. They usually have multiple rooms divided by a canvas wall, allowing for better privacy and storage. These tents are more compatible with larger groups, such as families or friends camping there.

Pros

- These tents are more spacious and taller, allowing you to move quickly and live comfortably.
- They often offer better storage space.
- These tents often can attach an awning or other attachments to create shade and wind protection.

Cons

- They require multiple people to set up.
- The large size and straight walls make the tent susceptible to strong winds blowing it over and in on itself.
- They take up a lot of packing space.

Geodesic Tents

Although small and compact, these tents are perfect for the experienced camper adventure in multiple climates. They are extremely well-adapted to be more stable than most other tent designs, thanks to the crisscrossing poles that form a geodesic pattern.

Pros

- These tents are highly stable; the poles create a self-supporting system that adds to their durability.
- Geodesic tents can withstand extreme weather conditions.
- The design allows the tent to be completely freestanding.

Cons

- These tents tend to be challenging to set up, and the pattern of the poles can make.
- them confusing. These tents are much heavier and bulkier, making them difficult to pack.
- They are usually quite expensive.
- These tents follow a dome-like shape, meaning there is little headroom.

Rooftop Tents

These tents are unique. Unlike other tents, these are entirely dependent on your vehicle. Although they offer unique benefits, they may not be suitable for families with small children or someone with mobility issues since they must be mounted on your vehicle.

Pros

- These tents offer better protection from the weather since you won't be camping on the ground.
- These tents are relatively easy to set up.
- You can camp anywhere if you can park your vehicle there.
- They are generally quick and easy to set up.

Cons

- These tents are usually expensive.
- They must be mounted on top of a vehicle, making it impossible to camp in certain areas.
- You need to be able to climb up into them.
- There is a risk of falling out of the tent.
- Although they offer better protection from cold and wet ground, they are susceptible to winds.

Pop-Up Tents

These tents are the perfect tents for a quick trip in perfect weather. They can also be used on the beach to provide shade and a haven for young kids. The best part about these tents is that their flexible poles are built in, so you don't need to carry them separately or figure out how to set them up. You will, however, must learn how to fold them again.

Pros

- These tents have a simple setup.
- They are usually lightweight and compact.

Cons

- They are highly susceptible to weather conditions.
- They are small and don't offer any storage space.

- They usually only come in a single-layer design, meaning these tents aren't breathable.

Bivouac Shelter

Like pop-up tents, these are small, compact, lightweight, and easy to use. But they also face the same problems. They use a bivy sack, as these tents are also known, along with a tarp to create a larger, breathable shelter., However, this means you must carry extra equipment, a tarp. Bivy sacks are usually small tunnels with one or two hoops to keep the material off your body, but they are just large enough for one adult to fit in.

Pros

- These tents are compact and lightweight.
- They are fast and easy to set up.

Cons

- They do not offer much space.
- They are not suitable for claustrophobic people.
- When zipped up, there is virtually no breathability room left.

Pyramid Tents

These tents are made from just one pole, which can double as a trekking pole and your cover. Unfortunately, this means this design could be more stable and comfortable. These tents do well in warm and dry climates when someone needs to pack something ultra-light and easy to carry, such as on an overnight hike. However, in other conditions, they are not preferred in the many guided lines and don't have a flooring material.

Pros

- These tents are very easy to set up.
- They are easy to pack since you only need to pack the tarp and can carry it as a trekking pole.

Cons

- The unstable structure makes the tent susceptible to falling in on itself under strong winds.
- The slanted walls allow water and debris to gather on the sides of the tent.
- The slanted walls create very little space inside the tent.
- There is no flooring.
- The center pole creates ineffective space usage and causes awkward sleeping positions.

#8—HAMMOCKS

One of the main aims of camping is to create a space where you can be comfortable and enjoy nature. Although tents are great for hiding from insects and the weather, you will also need somewhere to kick back and enjoy the sun and trees. That's where your hammock comes in. Hammocks are great for relaxing when you're not off adventuring or even for a nap under the stars when the weather allows it. Let's look at the different hammock options out there.

Single Hammocks

These are hammocks explicitly designed for one person. If you go on a solo adventure with little space, this might be the perfect hammock for you. The main issue with these hammocks is their weight limit; someone who might weigh a bit more than the average person will need to check if these hammocks can hold their weight.

Pros

- These compact and lightweight hammocks make them easy to pack and carry around.
- Single hammocks are often flexible regarding where they can be set up.
- They are typically simple to set up and usually include their suspension system.

- Being alone on a hammock can be more relaxing since you can decide when to swing, lay still, and be cozy.
- Single hammocks are cheaper and more affordable than any other hammock option.

Cons

- Single hammocks are not spacious, meaning you won't have much chance to spread out while sleeping.
- As mentioned earlier, these hammocks have weight limitations that don't always accommodate someone heavier.

Double Hammocks

These provide more space than a single hammock and are better equipped for more prominent people or two people sharing. Since they also come with a weight limit, you must check before using them.

Pros

- These hammocks are more spacious than single hammocks, allowing you to spread out more.
- They are great for sharing with a partner.

- Weight can be distributed more evenly, making the hammock more stable.
- They often come with storage pockets to keep your belongings close.

Cons

- Due to their larger size and weight than single hammocks, they are more challenging to store and carry.
- These hammocks require anchor points that are a lot stronger and more stable than those the single hammock requires.
- These hammocks can be more challenging to set up and require more adjustments during setup to achieve comfort and stability.
- Although they're not the most expensive hammock on the market, they are more expensive than single hammocks.

Family Hammock

These hammocks are large and can fit multiple people. They are great for a family with more minor children and can ensure your kids don't fall off while you are all down for an afternoon lounge and experiencing nature together.

Pros

- These hammocks boast much space, making them comfortable, and are also designed to be extremely strong and support much weight.

Cons

- Because of their massive size and weight, these hammocks take up much packing space and are heavy to carry around.
- These hammocks require strong anchor points, limiting where to set them up.
- These hammocks can be challenging to set up and require many adjustments while suspending them.
- They can be costly.

Spreader Bar Hammocks

These hammocks come in a variety of sizes and designs. They have a bar made of wood or metal on each side that spreads the fabric and allows for easier accessibility. You will prefer these hammocks if you spend much time on them.

Pros

- Because these hammocks don't envelope you as you climb on, they are much more accessible.

- The bars allow the hammock more stability than other variations.
- You enjoy a less disrupted view than you would if the hammock enveloped you.

Cons

- These hammocks can be much less comfortable than hammocks that conform to your shape.
- The bars cannot be collapsed, so the hammock requires more packing space.
- These hammocks also tend to be more expensive.

Classic Hammocks

These are the types of hammocks you are most likely used to. These hammocks have gathered ends instead of being spread out like other hammocks.

Pros

- These hammocks tend to conform to your shape the best, offering more comfort than other variations.
- Classic hammocks can be set up in various places and on more anchor points than most other variations.
- They are much lighter and more compact than other hammocks and take up less packing space.

- These also tend to be some of the most affordable hammocks.

Cons

- These hammocks may be somewhat tricky to set up at first.
- Although more comfortable, the enveloping effect means you will have less mobility inside the hammock and a limited view around you.
- Although these hammocks can use almost any anchor point, the anchor points must be highly stable.

Hammock Tents

Also known as camping hammocks, these hammocks are specifically designed to serve as your tent and usually come with a canopy that can be zipped up at night to keep the insects out. This makes them an excellent alternative to tents on an adventure where your packing space is minimal, but anchor points are definite.

Pros

- Camping hammocks are usually light and compact, which makes them easy to carry around and not take up a lot of packing space.

- Compared to other tents, you have more options for where to set up, as hammock tents don't require the ground to be dry or level.
- < UNK> Modern designs make setting these tents relatively easy.
- When using one of these, your impact on the environment is usually a lot less since you don't need to clear the ground for space, drive stakes into the ground, or kill any fauna you camp upon.

Cons

- These tents tend to have limited space as opposed to other tents, meaning you won't be able to keep supplies inside.
- Without the addition of other equipment, these tents tend to get a lot cooler than regular tents during the night and winter months.
- It might take a few tries to adjust the hammock to a comfortable position for you to sleep through the entire night.
- Hammock tents require good anchor points for set up, which means the tent cannot be used if your destination does not have these.

#9—CAMPING CHAIRS

Although hammocks are great for lounging and enjoying an afternoon nap, you will still need somewhere to sit, eat, or warm up next to the fire. This brings us to your camping chair, and once again, there are many more options than you might think.

Classic Camping Chairs

These chairs we commonly see have four legs connected to create a broad and stable base, including a backrest, flat seat, and armrests with cup holders.

Pros

- They provide comfortable seating.
- They are usually very stable.
- They can be folded up to be carried and packed more easily.
- They usually include at least one cup holder and sometimes even have storage compartments.

Cons

- Although they can be folded, they might still be bulky.
- They are heavier than other chairs.
- They can't be adjusted into other positions.

Low Chairs

These are also often referred to as beach chairs. They are low to the ground, which makes them perfect for sandy or uneven terrain. Although you can get canvas options, these chairs are usually plastic.

Pros

- Low chairs are incredibly lightweight and usually collapsible.
- They have increased stability on unstable ground, such as sandy terrain.

Cons

- These chairs have poor back support.
- They aren't very comfortable over a long period.
- They are unsuitable for people with mobility issues, such as someone with an injury or older adults.

Rockers

If you're anything like me, sitting still is difficult. These chairs are there for precisely this reason. This often makes them preferred for kids, as they can fidget and move around without damaging the chair. However, these chairs typically require a level ground.

Pros

- Rockers are more relaxing than other variations.
- Some of these chairs are collapsible.

Cons

- They tend to be heavier than other chairs.
- Even when collapsible, they can be bulky and difficult to store.
- They usually need a flat surface.

Hanging Chairs

Besides looking fabulous at your campsite, these pricey chairs have some functionality. By hanging them, you don't have to worry about the terrain or the chair falling over. They are suspended in the air using their frames, giving you a chance to have an excellent swing.

Pros

- Hanging chairs can be relaxing to swing in.
- They tend to be light and compact.
- They allow you to create seating in environments where the terrain may make it difficult.

Cons

- These chairs require an anchor point to be hung, which may not always be available.
- These chairs are unstable and will swing when the wind picks up, or you try to sit in them.

Three-Legged Chairs

These chairs include stools but can also be chairs with back-rests. Although they tend to be more compact and light-weight, they sacrifice stability for the design.

Pros

- Three-legged chairs are compact and lightweight, making them easier to transport and store.
- They are more stable than most other options.

Cons

- These chairs tend to be smaller than four-legged chairs.
- They can become uncomfortable over time.
- They usually require the level ground to be stable.

Two-Legged Chairs

These are different from my preferred style of chairs. Your feet are the front feet, so you must constantly use them to keep the chair upright. However, they have garnered some popularity due to their lightweight and reduced space usage. Just be careful not to fall backward.

Pros

- These chairs are lightweight and take up little space in storage and packing.
- They work much better for adventures requiring space-conscious packing, like camping without a car.

Cons

- They aren't stable at all.
- These chairs usually can't handle much weight, limiting who can use them.
- They become uncomfortable after a while.
- People with disabilities and mobility issues cannot use them.

#10—SLEEPING BAGS

Now that we have your shelter and seating arrangements sorted let's look at your sleeping situation. We'll start with your sleeping bags, which are the most important. They can be used in your tent, out in the open, and even in a hammock for added warmth. I'm sure it won't come as a surprise that, once again, there are many options. Let's have a look.

How to Pick Your Sleeping Bag

Before we get into the different sleeping bag designs, we need to look at the steps to choose your sleeping bag. This is quite important, as every design will also come in various temperature ratings and insulations, which will also affect the weight of your sleeping bag.

The first step is to decide what temperature sleeping bag you will require. If you don't plan on camping in the winter, you don't need a sleeping bag that will keep you warm at too-low temperatures. It would be best to keep in mind how your body typically operates. If you tend to get warm when you sleep, you don't need to look at a lower-temperature bag, whereas if you tend to get cold at night, you will need to look at one.

It is important to remember that the temperature rating of a sleeping bag means that it is the lowest temperature at which it will keep the average person warm. So, if a sleeping bag refers to a temperature rating of 10 degrees Fahrenheit, that is the coldest weather in which the average person can use this bag while remaining comfortable. You will need to use your judgment as to what temperature you will be kept warm at. Also, remember that when you feel too warm at night, you can easily unzip your sleeping bag for more ventilation, but when you are cold, you can't zip it up more.

Next, you will want to look at what insulation the sleeping bag offers. There are two different types of insulation to choose from down and synthetic. Each has its upside, as well as its downside.

Bags with down insulation provides better warmth than synthetic insulation, but unfortunately, some people are allergic to down. The other problem with the down is that it only works when wet. You can also get a different quality that affects how well it insulates. To check the quality of the down, look at its insulation specs, sometimes called fill power specs. The higher this number is, the better the down quality and the more warmth it offers you.

Synthetic insulation, on the other hand, works equally as well when wet as it does when dry, and you don't have the same chance of being allergic to it. Unfortunately, synthetic insulation does not compress well and tends to be heavier than sleeping bags.

Down sleeping bags also tend to last longer than synthetic sleeping bags. To counteract this, synthetic sleeping bags tend to be cheaper.

There is no right or wrong when choosing your insulation type. This is a choice to make based on your preferences and budget.

Lastly, look at the weight of your sleeping bag to determine whether it will suit your needs. If you plan on going back-packing or camping without a car, look at the lightweight options, but if you always plan on having a car with you, a heavier option may be a good idea. If weight is a deciding factor, compare the weight of the sleeping bags with others of the same temperature rating.

If you have looked at all these aspects, you are already close to choosing the perfect sleeping bag. All that remains is to look at the design you will need.

Rectangular Sleeping Bags

This is the most common type of sleeping bag you are most used to. They have a standard rectangular shape that can be zipped closed on one side, at the top, and on the bottom sometimes as well.

Pros

- This sleeping bag has a fair amount of room inside to move around.
- Some designs can be zipped open entirely to create a blanket on hot nights.

Cons

- They tend to be heavier than other designs.
- They tend to hold less heat, making them less effective in cold conditions.

Semi-Rectangular Sleeping Bags

These sleeping bags tend to be more tapered than ordinary rectangular sleeping bags.

Pros

- These sleeping bags retain more heat than their rectangular counterparts.

Cons

- Although more compact than ordinary rectangular sleeping bags, these sleeping bags are still somewhat heavy and space-consuming.

- They are still not the most effective heat retention in cold conditions.

Camping Quilts

These blanket-like systems are designed to be used with sleeping pads and do not come with full zippers or hoods.

Pros

- Camping quilts are lightweight and compact.
- They offer more movement freedom.
- They can be used as a blanket in warmer weather.
- They are easier to get into and out of than other designs.

Cons

- These quilts don't perform well in colder temperatures.
- They don't cover you as well as other sleeping bags do.
- They are specifically designed for sleeping pads and other equipment.

Mummy Sleeping Bags

The name explains these sleeping bags. They are designed to cover your entire body from head to toe. At the feet end, they have a tapered shape, while at the top, there is a hood.

Pros

- They have the best heat retention of any sleeping bag design.
- They are lightweight and compact.

Cons

- They can feel restrictive regarding movement, making this design incompatible with people with claustrophobia.
- They tend to be somewhat pricier.

Elephant Foot

These sleeping bags are designed to cover only your lower body and usually have a tapered design at the feet area. This design leaves your entire upper body free and exposed.

Pros

- These sleeping bags are perfect for summer camping trips and sitting next to the fire at night.
- They are incredibly lightweight and compact.

Cons

- They leave your upper body exposed.
- They are not suitable for cold nights at all.

Double Sleeping Bags

These sleeping bags are designed for two people who don't mind cuddling up at night. So, they are usually perfect for a couple.

Pros

- These sleeping bags are warmer since you have extra body heat.
- They are usually more affordable than buying two separate sleeping bags.

Cons

- They are heavy and bulky, making them hard to carry and store.
- There is a limited number of designs to choose from.

#11—SLEEPING PADS

A sleeping pad is another essential on our list. They offer protection from the ground, whether hard, uneven, or cold. They also offer back support to ensure you wake up feeling well-rested and good enough to face any adventure planned for the day. There are three different types of sleeping pads we'll investigate.

Air Sleeping Pads

These are the sleeping pads you are most familiar with. Think along the lines of an inflatable mattress. These sleeping pads are generally durable and have some material to help with insulation. They also come in various ways to be inflated, such as hand pumps or electronic pumps.

Pros

- The air inside the sleeping pad usually conforms to your body shape, adding comfort.
- These pads are usually lightweight and can be deflated and folded into a compact shape.
- You can adjust how firm your sleeping pad is by letting air out or pumping more in to ensure it suits your personal needs.
- They are generally quick and easy to inflate and deflate.

Cons

- They can develop air leaks or be punctured quite easily, causing them to deflate.
- They must be carefully stored and moved to ensure they are not damaged.
- Other types of sleeping pads offer better insulation.
- They can be noisy when you move around on them at night.

Closed-Cell Foam Sleeping Pads

These sleeping pads are made of a foam material that is usually quite dense and provides excellent insulation and cushioning. They usually come in a design that allows them to be rolled or folded.

Pros

- These sleeping pads are the most durable design as they don't suffer from air leaks.
- They can be packed exceptionally well and are easy to carry.
- They can be used on uneven and even rough terrain for support and insulation without fearing damage.

Cons

- They offer less support than other sleeping pad types.
- Their firmness cannot be adjusted.
- They are bulkier than air sleeping pads, causing them to take up more packing space.

Self-Inflating Sleeping Pads

These pads are a combination of inflatable and closed-cell sleeping pads. They usually have an air valve to let air in or out, depending on whether they should be inflated or deflated, and they don't require help inflating themselves.

Pros

- These sleeping pads are easy to set up; open and leave the air valve.
- They give a decent balance between comfort and insulation thanks to their combination design.
- They can still provide insulation when damaged.

Cons

- They are heavier and bulkier than other types, taking the most amount of packing space.
- They may take a while to inflate themselves fully.

- They can still lose air due to damage, leading to a need for repair or replacement.

#12—PILLOWS

So, thus far, we have sorted out most of your sleeping arrangements. Now you should be comfortable and warm. But your sleeping position might still feel like it could be more comfortable. You won't get proper neck support without a pillow, leading to neck pain. We don't want this happening as neck pain and the poor night's sleep that will surely accompany it can damper our holidays. So, let's look at the available pillow choices you have for camping.

Inflatable

Much like inflatable sleeping pads, you can get inflatable pillows as well. If an inflatable sleeping pad is your preferred choice, you will often see inflatable pillows of the same design.

Pros

- They are lightweight and compact and can be deflated and folded into small objects.
- They are relatively easy to use; most are small enough to be blown up with your breath.

Cons

- They can be uncomfortable as most designs are made from plastic materials.
- They tend to make noise as you move during the night.
- They are susceptible to damage that can cause leakage.

Compressible

These pillows will remind you of the pillows you have in your bedroom, with one key difference: they come with a compression pack that allows you to squeeze them flat, making them easier to pack than your bedroom pillows. These pillows also usually have similar materials to ours to never damage, such as down, foam, or synthetic fibers.

Pros

- Compressible pillows aren't prone to damage that can cause them to deflate.
- They are more comfortable than inflatable pillows.

Cons

- These pillows can only compress so much, which takes up more space than other options.

- They can lose their firmness over time.

Hybrid

These pillows combine the inflatable pillow with a compressible top. This allows them to be quite comfortable and offer much support while being more compact and accessible to carry than compressible pillows.

Pros

- Hybrid pillows have better support for your head.
- They are more adjustable with less impact on comfort when being adjusted.
- They take the least storage space compared to your other options.

Cons

- When damaged, they are still susceptible to leaking air.

#13—BLANKETS

I know what you're thinking; why would you need a blanket and a sleeping bag? It can get extremely cold out in the wilderness; you never know what can happen. A sleeping bag is sufficient to keep most of the cold at bay, but you will need your blanket to warm up properly. Regarding blankets, the material will be the most crucial aspect you need to look at.

Wool

Wool blankets are highly effective, so they are still popularly used worldwide. You can also choose from several different types of wool, opening your options quite a bit.

Pros

- Wool blankets are usually fire-resistant.
- Wool is a moisture-wicking material, drawing moisture out to the surface.
- There is a variety of different types of wool to choose from.
- Wool continues to offer insulation even when wet.

Cons

- Wool is not very comfortable.
- It takes a long time to dry.
- It is cumbersome and bulky, making it difficult to carry and store.

Plastic

I highly recommend camping with one of these blankets, even if you have everything else. These lightweight and compact blankets are great in emergencies. Of course, if you only go out for a single night, you should use one instead of carrying around a bulkier alternative.

Pros

- Plastic blankets are designed to trap heat.
- They are lightweight and compact.
- They are easy to use.
- They are perfect for emergencies.

Cons

- They are not very durable and only last for a few uses.
- They are not very comfortable.

Polyester

These synthetic blankets come with various perks and are perfect for all types of weather. If you choose a polyester blanket, ensure you never put it in the dryer, as this can cause it to shrink.

Pros

- Polyester blankets are both waterproof and fire-resistant.
- They are lightweight, making them easy to carry around.
- They are warm and even work well for insulation when wet.
- They are very durable.
- They are comfortable.
- They are quick-drying.

Cons

- High heat, such as that from a dryer, can cause the blanket to shrink.

Fleece

This is the synthetic version of a wool blanket, perfect for those who don't use products made from animal by-products.

Pros

- Fleece blankets are very good at insulating.
- They are lightweight, making them easy to carry.
- They are quick to dry.

Cons

- Fleece is a highly flammable material, so you won't be able to use it near a fire.

HYGIENE KITS

Now that we've covered everything you need to ensure you have a safe and warm campsite to enjoy, we need to cover hygiene. I believe it's fair to say that we all prefer to be clean. When camping, however, you are constantly climbing something, walking somewhere, or just getting dirt everywhere without knowing how. To ensure you are always clean and presentable and can enjoy your trip without cutting it short to take a shower, here is a list of essentials you need for your hygiene kit.

#14—Unscented Alcohol-Based Hand Sanitizer

When you are out on the trails, climbing rocks, or enjoying nature all day, you never realize how much you touch around you. Since this is the wilderness, the surfaces, and objects you touch must be cleaned. Having a bottle of alcohol-based hand sanitizer with you ensures you can clean off any germs on your hands. I specifically mention unscented sanitizer as animals rely heavily on their sense of smell, and you never know how they will react to the smell of your sanitizer.

#15—Biodegradable Soap

We all think that because soap cleans, it must be clean *and* safe, right? Not necessarily. Ordinary soap that you would use at home, including your hand, body, and dish, can damage the fragile ecosystems found in national parks. This is why we use biodegradable soap in the wilderness, free from added chemicals that will damage the environment. Please remember that even if you use biodegradable soap, ensure it does not come within 200 feet of a natural water source. It can still cause much damage to the ecosystem.

#16—Toothbrush

Your dental hygiene is essential. Always take your toothbrush with you and keep your teeth clean so they don't deteriorate.

#17—Toothpaste

When you take toothpaste, ensure it has no fancy smells or additives and is essential. Remember, when you brush your teeth, don't spit your toothpaste out into a water source; instead, spit it into your fire pit. This is a piece of ground you have already disturbed and will continue to do so throughout your stay.

#18—Dental Floss

As I've said, don't miss out on dental hygiene just because you are roughing it. Always make sure you are flossing. Also, if you are in a tough spot and need a piece of string, your floss might be the quick fix you are looking for.

#19—Washcloth

When we are out in the wilderness all day, regardless of the weather, you will probably end up sweating and getting dirty everywhere, and I mean everywhere. There is no better way to get sweat and sand off your body than with a washcloth. A washcloth also helps you use less soap and water while cleaning, thereby slightly preserving the area.

#20—Unscented Moist Towelettes

You will cut yourself, touch something that you may not want to know what it is and get all sorts of things stuck all over your body. These might be things you don't necessarily want to use your hands or washcloth to remove, and that is where moist towelettes come in handy.

#21—Quick-Dry Microfiber Pack Towel

Instead of bringing your regular home towel that you will need to pack away while still wet or leave out to dry for hours, where it can pick up more dirt, get a quick-dry microfiber towel. This allows you to dry yourself off and pack your towel away again without worrying that it might start to smell from the trapped moisture or that some wild animal might get to it while you are off on an adventure.

#22—Toilet Paper

Toilet paper is essential for a variety of reasons. Not only for your specific hygiene purposes, it can also be used to clean off other objects in a pinch. When you use toilet paper, there is one downside. You must keep the toilet paper in a disposable bag until you can safely remove it to ensure it has no environmental impact.

#23—Portable Camping Shower Bag

These are a great addition to any camper's adventure, especially if you plan to camp in more remote areas. When there are no showers available, you can use this little shower bag to ensure the dirt is removed from your body, using very little water. Some of them are also designed to be used in direct sunlight to allow the water to heat up so that you don't have an icy cold shower.

#24—Disposable Bags

Your disposable bag is for yourself and the environment's hygiene. Anything you use should be discarded in a disposable bag until you can dispose of it properly in a designated bin or dumpster area where it will not affect the environment. If you can, biodegradable disposable bags are the best option, especially for dry refuse.

CLOTHING

During the previous chapter, we spoke a lot about different clothing for each season, but we'll now look deeper into what those clothing items are. Before we do that, however, there are some clothing options you should avoid at all costs on a camping adventure.

These options are:

- Expensive clothing and accessories
- Cotton and denim
- White clothing
- Open-toed shoes

Now that we have that out, we can investigate what we should take.

Summer and Spring

Let's start with clothing for the warmer months of the year. In summer and spring, you will most often wear similar clothing.

#25—Moisture-Wicking Clothes

You should be used to the term moisture-wicking by the time you finish this book. During the heat, this high-tech polyester clothing will be your best friend as it absorbs the sweat and moisture from your body and helps you cool down.

#26—Sun Hat

The sun can become quite scorching during these two months, so a sun hat is required to protect your face from the possibly harmful rays of the sun. You can also take various hats to be comfortable and protected.

#27—Quick-Drying Socks

As mentioned, you should not wear open-toed shoes while on a camping trip. This is a safety concern, but you will probably always wear socks. When you wear socks, they are guaranteed to get wet when you pass a stream or trek through mud. Get quick-drying socks to ensure you are comfortable and dry at all times. This also means you don't have to worry about putting away still-wet or damp socks that will start to smell and grow their ecosystems.

#28—Quick-Drying Shorts and Pants

Just like with your socks, there is a good chance your pants will get wet by walking through water, rain, or mud. To stay warm and safe, your clothing should be able to dry out quickly.

#29—Just-In-Case Warm Clothing

As we've established, the weather can change quickly, especially during the springtime. But even in summer, the temperature can drop relatively low at night, depending on the terrain around you. So, to ensure you are protected in cold weather, take extra clothing that you can layer.

#30—Rain Jacket

Spring and summertime usually bring rain with them. To keep yourself warm and dry, you must have a jacket that can protect you from the wind and rain.

#31—Swimsuit

When it's not raining, and the park allows it, you will want to get away from the sun and into the nearest body of water to enjoy the cool, natural water. It won't be a good idea to do it in your hiking clothes, and since there will probably be other families, skinny dipping is also not an option. This is where your swimsuit comes in.

#32—Water Shoes

Whether hiking, fishing, kayaking, or exploring water in some other way, you already know you will get wet. Water shoes have drainage holes that allow all the water to get out while also being quick-drying. This means you can enjoy the water without worrying that your shoes will take hours to dry out.

Fall and Winter

The temperature drops in fall and winter, and your clothing options must change. You go from enjoying the sun and staying dry to preserving the heat at all costs and staying warm. So, here are the clothing options to look at during these two seasons.

#33—Winter Hats

While sun hats are meant to keep the sun at bay so your face and neck do not get burned, winter hats are designed to keep the heat in so that your ears, head, and sometimes face remain warm and safe at all times.

#34—Layers

During the winter and fall, the temperature is guaranteed to fall to some low levels, especially at night. To protect your-self, investigate wearing clothing that can be layered on each other to give you the maximum heat but can still be removed when the temperature rises.

#35—Wool Socks

Wool is one of the most effective insulators and best at keeping your feet and legs warm. During winter months especially, long wool socks are of the utmost importance.

#36—Gloves

You will need gloves to protect your fingers and retain dexterity so you can more easily make fire, climb rocks, and use your hands. They will keep your hands warm and even help keep your body temperature slightly higher in the cold.

#37—Waterproof Jackets

There is nothing worse than getting wet when it's cold. Waterproof jackets are like rain jackets but offer better insulation and wind protection. These are specifically designed for winter conditions where you might be exposed to snow or water in any form.

#38—Waterproof Shoes

While water shoes allow water to get in and dry quickly, they won't work well in winter as they will cause the temperature of your feet to drop quite severely when wet and could even lead to frostbite. This is why you will need shoes that keep water away from your feet during the winter and fall.

#39—Quick-Dry Clothing

As I've already said, nothing is worse than getting wet when it's cold. However, chances are that at some point, something will happen, and you will find yourself wet. When this happens, your priority will be to get warm and dry as quickly as possible. To help with this process, quick-dry clothing is essential.

SO, WHAT DO WE KNOW?

This has been a bulky chapter, but we've gotten through the most basic requirements to have a safe and temperature-controlled camping site, from our shelter to where we relax and sleep. We know what to wear and how to stay clean. Now, it's time to look at the tools and equipment needed to make our shelters a home away from home.

4

CAMPING HARDWARE, EQUIPMENT, AND TOOLS

The next group of essentials we will need to investigate is the hardware, tools, and equipment we will need on our adventures. These items will help you with everything from getting to and preparing your campsite to your adventures.

HARDWARE

Let's start by looking at the physical tools used during your adventures.

#40—Knives

There is a wide variety of knives for you to choose from. Each has its uses and benefits, and you are always welcome to take more than one type of knife. Just be sure to check your destination's local laws, as some of these blades may be illegal, especially if you are flying.

Pocketknife

These small knives can be used for minor tasks, like cutting meat, cutting string, or dislodging something stuck. These knives are not the strongest and can break if too much pressure is on them, but they are great when you need something small and simple. They are helpful as the blade can be folded into the handle, making the entire object compact and small.

Clip-Folder

These are like pocketknives but tend to be a bit larger and have a clip attached to the handle so that they can rest on your belt or outside your pocket. This way, you have quick and easy access to the knife, and since it is larger, it is also suited for more uses.

Assist-Opening

These knives work similarly to the previous two we've discussed. Still, their significant difference is that while the other two knives must be unfolded manually, this one will spring open entirely or partially, depending on its design. This makes the assist-opening perfect for emergency conditions where you quickly need to get a blade and might not always have a clear field of vision.

Survival Knife

This knife is top-rated since it is designed for use in the wilderness during survival situations. These knives are designed to be durable and robust; they should be able to cut through wood without many problems. They also often have hollow handles that can store emergency items, such as something to start a fire with.

Machete

I was reluctant to put this on the list, but since we value safety, the machete does have its place. The machete is best used to cut through thick vegetation, which means it causes the most amount of harm to the environment. If you want to ensure you leave no trace while camping, the machete will not do that. However, the machete will be the most effective in an emergency where you must travel quickly or cut yourself out of a situation. If you bring a machete with you on a camping trip, please, only take it out in case of an emergency.

#41—Axes

While the different types of axes don't make much of a difference besides durability, there is a large variety of uses for an axe on a camping trip that we'll need to explore. Also, of course, due to the power of this tool, we cannot gloss over it without a few safety precautions.

The Uses of an Axe While Camping

Wood Chopping

This is, of course, the exact purpose the ax had been designed for. However, do not cut down or cut wood from any trees in a national park. You might be allowed to cut up some of the already-fallen dead wood, but you should check with the park officials first.

Tinder and Kindling

Some of the essential ingredients in a fire are your tinder and kindling. You can use your ax to make this by chopping your firewood into smaller bits.

Hammer

The flat rear end of your ax can be used as a hammer when you don't have any other suitable tool.

Emergency Situations

There is always a chance that something will go wrong. When this happens, your ax has two primary purposes: the first is to help you build a shelter, and the second is to use the blade to reflect light when you need to do emergency signaling.

Safety Regulations

There are a few rules to follow when you take an ax with you on a camping trip to ensure that you and your fellow campers remain safe.

1. Always ensure your blade is sharp. A dull blade is more prone to causing recoil, which can lead to injury.
2. When your ax is not used, it should be covered with a sheath.
3. When using an ax, keep a fair distance from other people and habitable places. This reduces the risk of hitting someone accidentally and ensures that splinters and broken pieces of wood don't end up in someone's feet or puncture equipment.
4. ensure you have a proper grip and stance when using your ax. This reduces the risk of losing control over the ax.
5. When not using your ax, secure it somewhere safe and out of the way. That way, nobody will get hurt, and it will remain out of children's reach.

#42—Multi-Tool

A multi-tool is like a folding knife, with the significant difference being that it has several different tools, ranging from a knife to a nail file, a bottle opener, screwdrivers, a pair of pliers, and a few others. These are always great to have with you since they are compact and designed to fit in your pocket or your belt. Multi-tools have a few pros and cons to them:

Pros

- These tools are compact and lightweight and can be carried in your pocket without causing discomfort.
- Multi-tools save space instead of carrying around several tools.
- The different tools make it multifunctional.
- There is less chance of losing specific tools.

Cons

- You can only use one tool at a time.
- They are good at basic tasks but will not perform well in specialized tasks.
- It is tough to get leverage.

#43—Shovel

There are only two types of shovels: a standard, straightforward shovel and a multipurpose shovel. These are your choices. It may seem simple to grab a multipurpose and move on. Well, yes and no. Multipurpose shovels are pricier, and if you already have the tools, then spending all that money may be a good use. On the other hand, most multi-purpose camping shovels are lightweight, compact, and can fold into smaller shapes to take up less space. Also, having redundancy is a good thing.

#44—Carabiner

If you're not entirely sure what this word means, don't worry. I also didn't know what a carabiner was for the longest time until I saw a picture of it and realized I had several as part of my camping tools for as long as I have been camping.

A carabiner is a curved coupling hook with a straight bar that acts as a gate and usually opens inward. We may use it as a keyring or holder for some objects in everyday life. I have three of them hanging in my kitchen, holding portable hand sanitizers. This speaks to the versatility of the carabiner. However, the carabiner shines when it gets to the great outdoors.

Let's look at how we can use this handy little object out in the wild.

Belt Clip

A carabiner can easily attach to your belt and the loops on your pants through which your belt goes. Once there, you can attach various objects, such as your water bottle, tools, and anything with a hooped string or ring.

Organizers

Your carabiner can keep random small items that generally find their way to the bottom of your backpack organized. These would be items like multi-tools and flashlights. Most backpacks will allow you to attach the carabiner to the outside, allowing easier access to these objects and more space inside the bag.

Locking Mechanism

When you are not using a carabiner to carry something, you can use it as a makeshift locking mechanism for your bags and containers. This will keep them from jumping open when being carried around and even keep animals out of them.

Quick-Release Connections

Carabiners are designed not just to allow you to connect objects securely but also to be able to release them quickly and efficiently when necessary. This saves you from cutting apart your expensive hammock or tarp in emergencies.

Makeshift Pulleys

A pulley system can make your life a lot easier. Some parks suggest keeping your food suspended from a tree at night or when you leave camp so that animals cannot easily access them. This is where a carabiner comes in. Using it as a pulley can make moving objects or suspending them in the air much more accessible.

#45—Ropes

There are many types of ropes, each with its place and uses on camping trips. Of course, taking every type of rope with you might not be possible, but if you have some with you, it shouldn't be a problem. The ropes are mentioned in order of the best to the worst for camping.

Paracord

These lightweight ropes were designed for use in parachutes, as their name suggests. Again, they have found their way onto the list of camping essentials because of their impressive strength and durability. Due to their purpose, these ropes are also closely regulated, so you know they are guaranteed to be of excellent quality.

Climbing Rope

This rope was explicitly made for climbing but can be used for other purposes. This rope consists of an inner and outer section called a kern mantle design. The inner rope is made of a solid material that allows the rope to carry impressive weights. In contrast, the outer rope is made of a solid abrasion-resistant material that allows the rope to be more durable than most other types.

Baling Twine

This is the rope that farmers use to tie up their hay bales, which means it is pretty strong while still affordable. It still does not compare to paracord or climbing rope in strength and durability, but it beats them in affordability for one-time uses.

Twisted/Laid Rope

This relatively cheap rope is usually made from three strands twisted together. This rope is relatively cheap, making it the perfect rope to cut up when needed. The biggest drawback of these ropes is that they tend to kink easily and are far from the most robust rope.

Guyline Cord

This rope is less solid and durable than climbing ropes or paracords. But they have a thoughtful design that makes them perfect for setting up tarps or tents because you won't trip over the rope at night. However, I would not suggest using it on anything meant to hold weight, such as your hammock.

Sisal Rope

This is the final rope type we will look at. This rope is made of natural fibers and is highly resistant to the corrosive effects of saltwater. Unfortunately, it also can cut your hands quite easily. It is solid and inexpensive to make up for that.

Six Important Knots

Now that we know what ropes are available, we must look at the six most essential knots any camper should know. Because of the complex nature of knots, I'll give you the name of the knots but invite you to look up online tutorials on making them and practice before going on your first adventure.

1. Sheet bend
2. Bowline knots
3. Two half stitches
4. Taut line
5. Clove hitch
6. Square knot

#46—Duct Tape

We all know duct tape. It sticks to anything and everything, and it is solid. This is why duct tape should be essential for any camper. You never know when you might need it and what you might need it for. Here are some examples of how to use duct tape on your camping trip.

Tent Repairs

From a tear in your tent's material to fixing a broken pole and even keeping your tent closed if the zipper broke or it came without a zipper—almost anything that goes wrong with your tent can temporarily be fixed with duct tape.

Sleeping Bags and Pads

If your sleeping bag or pad suffers damage, you can use duct tape to keep it together to survive your trip until you return. Duct tape might not always be perfect for keeping your sleeping pads airtight, but it can at least slow the leak so you don't wake up on the ground halfway through the night.

Camping Chairs

We've already established that tears are no match for duct tape. So, keep your camping chair working with well-placed duct tape for the rest of your trip.

Fly Traps

During the summer, flies can be a real pain in the backside, but by hanging a strip of duct tape in your camping area, you can easily create a fly ribbon that catches the flies and keeps them off you.

Seal Packets

Whether you want to keep your disposable bag sealed until you can get rid of it or seal food packets, so the insides stay fresh and the smell doesn't attract unwanted visitors, duct tape is your friend.

#47—Batteries and Generators

We've become reliant on electricity, whether charging our cell phones or switching on a flashlight. Even in the wilderness, we take power with us. That's not necessarily bad, as it can mean we are a lot safer when we can see better and share our location with others in an emergency. Electricity has its upside.

Benefits of a Generator During Camping

Before you pack your generator and head off into the wild, ensure your camping destination allows generators. These noisy machines can cause discomfort for other guests and animals, not to mention the air pollution from them and the fire hazard they pose. Due to these factors, many national parks have banned using a generator. If your park allows a generator, though, there are benefits you can enjoy. However, you will want to make sure that you use a portable camping generator. These generators tend to be quieter and less intrusive than the ones we use in the city. And while those big gas generators are usually banned, the smaller camping generators are almost always accepted. Here are the benefits of using a generator:

- You will have access to electricity even when no power outlets are available.
- Nights can be much more comfortable with warm drinks and ample lighting.

- They reduce risks while camping in remote areas.
- Camping generators tend not to bother your neighbors or the animals.

Benefits of Batteries During Camping

When discussing batteries during camping, it's easy to get confused and think we are referring to the batteries you put in a flashlight. While it is always recommended that you carry spare batteries like those, the batteries we refer to here are a bit larger and capable of running your camping equipment, like a small fridge and lights. These camping battery systems can be a life changer; the difference is between roughing and enjoying it to the fullest. They also come with their own set of benefits:

- They provide a source of backup power if no power is available.
- Some batteries can be connected to a solar system.
- They can power various devices, from your phone to your RV.
- They are usually lightweight and compact.
- They are available in many different sizes you can choose from to fit your specific power needs.
- They usually last quite a long time before needing to be recharged.

#48—Fire Starter

Fire is such an essential part of camping that it is almost inconceivable for us to go camping without some way of starting a fire. Sitting around the fire at night, telling stories, and just spending time with each other is almost seen as a requirement of camping. So, to ensure you have access to this beautiful experience, you must have some fire-starting equipment.

The Benefits of a Fire Starter While Camping

- It makes starting a fire quick and easy each time.
- It can start a fire in wet conditions.
- Fire can be the difference between life and death in an emergency.
- Fires and fire starters can provide light when needed.
- Fire can be used to purify water.
- Fire can be used to create signals in emergencies.

Pros and Cons of Matches and Lighters

The most common fire starters are matches (usually water-proof) and lighters. I suggest ensuring you have both when camping, as one tends to work when the other doesn't. For example, a lighter can be used when it's raining, whereas a match can't. However, a lighter might not ignite in freezing conditions, whereas a match will. At the same time, a lighter can be used hundreds of times before the fluid runs out, while a box of matches can only be used a handful of times until the matches are finished. A lighter also usually has the benefit of being refillable.

In the end, when you have both types of fire starters with you, you have a whole lot of pros and no cons. Luckily, both options take up a little space.

#49—Lights

When camping in a national park, seeing where you go at night is essential. It's important because you can easily trip over a rock or a line and because there are also wild animals and insects lurking about, such as snakes or spiders.

You must also ensure you can find your way and know your location. To do this, you will need several different types of light. Most of these lights come with an LED option that is more energy efficient and can create brighter lights than other varieties. The following lights are essential to your safety and enjoyment of your camping adventure.

Headlamp

A headlamp is especially helpful on fishing trips but can be used when you need to complete a task that requires both hands. The light will automatically be focused toward the area you are facing, and since you don't need to hold on to it, your hands are freed up.

Hand Light

These lights are larger and heavier than headlamps, which usually means they are brighter and have a more extended range. These lights are perfect if you need to see what is happening around you or to guide someone around at night.

Lantern

You can get various portable LED lanterns, most rechargeable and some even solar-powered. These lanterns provide constant light in areas where your campfire can't, such as inside your tent. You can also hang them in the trees on the outskirts of your camp to ensure the entire camp has visibility.

Ground Light

These lights are often bulkier and more considerable than lanterns but provide much more light. They are usually used in areas where tasks are done to ensure complete visibility, such as where you want to prepare dinner.

Campfire

No camp is complete without a campfire. This is not just essential; it is a requirement. Luckily, you already have the tools required to make this great source of light, heat, and ambiance.

Keyring Light

These lights are more for when you are in a pinch and don't need something as big or focused as a headlamp or hand light. Instead, you can clip these lights to your carabiner to always have some light within arm's reach. These lights don't usually last very long, so they should be used sparingly.

Glow Sticks

This is another "in case of emergency" light. Glow sticks are not eco-friendly and can be dangerous to animals, especially if they find them unattended and try to eat them. On the other hand, these are extremely good in emergencies to create visibility around you. If you use a glow stick, dispose of it properly when you are done.

HIKING GEAR

Hiking is a large part of camping. To enjoy the national park, you are visiting its fullest. You will probably find yourself hiking to some of its attractions. So, to not only enjoy your hike but finish it like a pro, there are a few things that you should always have with you.

#50—Navigation Devices

The first items in your hiking gear should be items for navigation. This is important so you know where you are going while hiking, but these items can also help you find your way if you get lost.

GPS Devices

We live in modern times where some satellite is almost always hovering over us. So, use this to your benefit. GPS devices are unique and can make navigation very simple. This is why they are your number one essential when hiking.

Compass

I can already hear the question: "Why would I need a compass if I have a smartphone and a GPS device?" Well, what will you do when these run out of power? As great as technology has gotten, it still has flaws, and we must always have a backup plan. Using a compass and remembering your destination, you can easily find your way home again.

Regional Maps

Once again, this is a tech-free alternative to a GPS device that can save your life when all else fails. It might also be a good idea to take a few lessons on reading a map before you leave on your adventure. This way, you are assured that you will be safe and always find your way back even if something happens and you become lost or turned around.

#51—Trekking Poles

The purpose of a trekking pole is always to have some form of support and stability while hiking. Many people refuse to use trekking poles because they think only older adults or those with mobility issues need them. This is a big mistake; a trekking pole is a must-have for everyone. In a moment, we'll investigate the uses of a trekking pole, but first, let's look at how to choose your trekking pole.

You will first need to decide whether you want a single hiking staff or a pair of poles for extra support on both sides. There is no wrong answer, and you should choose the option that is most comfortable for you.

Once you have done this, you must find a pole with the correct length. Luckily, some trekking pole designs allow you to adjust their length. The ideal length for a trekking pole will have the tip of the pole touch the ground when your elbow is at a 90-degree bend.

Lastly, choose a trekking pole that has features you prefer. This will include length adjustment, folding up, and shock absorption. When you have chosen the perfect pole for you, moving through rugged, uneven terrain littered with obstacles will be a breeze.

Different Uses Outside of Hiking

Some trekking poles can be used for more than just mobility. These are usually made possible with add-on features. Let's see what you can use your trekking pole for:

- **Shelter:** You can easily create a makeshift shelter in need using your trekking pole and a tarp.
- **Photography:** You can quickly turn your trekking pole into a selfie stick or monopod through some add-on features or self-made makeshift adjustments.
- **First aid:** A trekking pole can be used to make a splint and a stretcher if you find yourself in a pinch.
- **Probing:** Your trekking pole can probe the depth of water, snow, and mud to inform you if walking in a particular area is safe.
- **Communication:** When you find yourself in an emergency, the length of the pole makes it easier for you to be seen from the air, and by banging it against other objects, you can make noise that can help others find you.

#52—Bug Spray

One thing we can be assured of in the wild is that we will encounter some bugs during the middle of winter or summer. As humans, we often don't like bugs and would prefer it if they stayed away from us, as far away as possible.

That is why humans have created bug sprays or insect repellants. These beautiful creations come in various options based on the active ingredient that keeps bugs away from you.

Permethrin

This insect repellent is unique because it is not meant to come in direct contact with human skin. Instead, you can purchase clothing that has been pretreated with this chemical or purchase the chemical in spray form to use on your clothing and camping equipment. This repellent lasts for a few weeks and should be sprayed onto your gear a day or two before traveling so it has enough time to dry properly.

DEET-Based

This is seen as the best of the best when it comes to insect repellents. DEET-based repellents are effective against mosquitoes, ticks, fleas, and some flies. This repellent was developed by the United States military, which speaks to its level of quality. These repellents can be found in various concentrations ranging from 5% to 100%; however, there is little change in effectiveness above 30%.

This repellent comes in lotion, spray, and wipe form and lasts between 6 and 12 hours. The risk of allergy with this repellent is also shallow, although not unheard of.

The main drawbacks of DEET-based repellents are that they can damage synthetic fibers, are not safe for children under two months, and cannot be used for a prolonged time as they can cause adverse side effects.

Catnip Oil

This is a more natural insect repellent made of a catnip plant in the mint family. Surprisingly, this oil has been recorded as being up to ten times more effective than DEET-based insect repellents. The oil is applied directly to your skin and is quite effective against flies and mosquitoes. Other than eye irritation, there are no other reported side effects either.

Picaridin

Picaridin is a synthetic chemical, much like the natural chemicals found in black pepper. Picaridin-based repellents are available in concentrations ranging from 5% to 20% and come in spray and wipes.

The spray variant of these repellents has been found to work better than some DEET-based repellents. Another advantage of these repellents is that they do not cause damage to synthetic fibers and make your skin less sticky. Lastly, they tend to last longer than some other repellent variants.

AR3535

These repellents are available as a lotion and a spray with concentrations between 7.5% and 20%. These are more suited for summer and spring as they are usually sold with sunscreen. However, the downside is that sunscreen needs to be applied more often than insect repellents, and using excessive amounts of insect repellent can have adverse side effects. Other than that, some serious questions have been raised regarding the effectiveness of these repellents with only a 7.5% concentration.

BioUD

Made from wild tomato plants, this synthetic repellent is not highly toxic. The repellent is effective against mosquitos and ticks, albeit only briefly. Generally, BioUD repellents will repel mosquitoes for around six hours and ticks for only two and a half hours, making its reapplication necessary.

Citronella

Citronella is a rather popular form of insect repellent and can be found in the most extensive array of varieties. It comes in sprays, wristbands, candles, and even incense. That being said, citronella works by hiding the scent that would typically attract an insect to you and can be used to clear areas of insects instead of stopping insects from biting you. Citronella can also irritate your skin, eyes, and throat and should not be used on children younger than six months.

Lemon Eucalyptus

Although often marketed as a natural insect repellent, this is only a plant-based repellent. This means that it can cause skin irritations and be toxic when swallowed. It is also recommended that you do not use these repellents on children under the age of nine years. Aside from all this, these repellents were found only to be effective for about six hours, and even then, they are only as effective as lower-concentration DEET products.

#53—Camping Tarps

We've discussed camping tarps quite a bit, but let's look at what a camping tarp is. As you may have gathered by now, a tarp is usually a large piece of durable and waterproof material that can be used in various ways. Let's start by looking at the benefits of a tarp.

Shelter

A tarp can be used to create shelter in calm weather conditions. Using a tarp and your trekking pole together, you can quickly create a basic shelter to hide from the sun and rain. Aside from that, you can create a large, sheltered area like a gazebo using guy lines and anchor points.

Additional Protection

If you already have a shelter constructed, a tarp can increase your shelter's protection from rain and wind. You can even use a tarp under your shelter for additional protection from the cold, moisture, or wet ground underneath your shelter.

Endless Possibilities

A tarp can be used for a wide variety of things. Aside from what we have covered, your tarp can be used as a picnic blanket, makeshift stretcher, windbreak, and many other functional items.

Lightweight and Compact

Tarps are usually lightweight and compact and can be folded to take up less space. This gives you quite a good reason to pack at least one tarp wherever you go.

Cost-Effective

Tarps are usually affordable, and when you compare their prices to their uses, they are highly cost-effective.

Cons of Tarps

Just as with anything else, a tarp does have its downsides.

- It only offers limited protection from the elements, mainly when used alone.
- When used to create shelter, the shelter is fundamental and may not be stable or provide much privacy.
- Setting up a tarp can be tricky and complex.

- Using a tarp as additional protection from the
  elements can decrease the breathability of a shelter.

SO, WHAT DO WE KNOW?

At last, we have everything we will need to go on a camping trip and even have adventures there. We've almost got all our basics covered. This chapter has ensured that you have all the necessary camping and adventure tools. But there is always the risk of something going wrong, so let's look into emergencies.

CAMPING FOR ALL!

"Wilderness is not a luxury but a necessity of the human spirit."

— *EDWARD ABBEY*

Camping is such an affordable and practical way to take a break from the stress of everyday life, yet for many people, the idea either doesn't register, or they don't have a clue what they'd need to do to take advantage of all it has to offer.

Yet it's such an easy and fulfilling way to get back to nature, gain perspective, and spend time with friends and family while the pressures of the working week melt away.

As mentioned in the introduction, I've seen so many people give up at the first hurdle that it's become very important to me to share the skills and knowledge I've been sitting on all these years… and now that you're adding that knowledge to your toolbox too, you're in the perfect position to help me.

Don't worry – I'm not asking you to run a workshop or hand out pamphlets… I only need a few moments of your time. Without leaving your living room, you can help me get the word out and make camping accessible to even more people.

By leaving a review of this book on Amazon, you'll show hopeful campers where they can find everything they need to know to pack their tents with confidence and start a new way of life with regular escapes into nature.

Simply by letting new readers know how this book has helped you and what they'll find inside, you'll point them in the direction of all the knowledge they need to set out on their first camping trip with confidence – and as you'll know yourself very soon, they'll never look back.

Thank you for your support. Learning how to camp opens up a treasure trove of regular vacations – and I want to make sure that's available to everyone.

5

PREPARING FOR EMERGENCIES

One of our biggest concerns throughout the book so far has been safety. On more than one occasion, I've referenced possible emergencies and how to prepare for them, and that is because the rules of life say that somewhere along the line, something will always go wrong. It's not a question of if but a question of when, and all we can do is ensure that we are as prepared as we can be when something inevitably happens.

#54—FIRST AID KIT

The first step in preparing for an emergency is having all the necessary tools. All the tools for emergencies will be in your first aid kit. That is why it is essential for any adventure. Before you leave for an adventure, you need to check, double-check, and check once more that your first aid kit is fully stocked and packed for your trip.

The Benefits of a First Aid Kit

- You will be able to respond to injuries immediately.
- Early treatment can lower the chances of infection, usually higher in outdoor environments.
- You can have pain relief and comfort while waiting for better treatment.
- Having a first aid kit can give you and your fellow campers peace of mind.
- Some destinations and activities require you to have a first aid kit on hand before allowing you to participate.

Items That Should Be in Your First Aid Kit

The following items should always be in your first aid kit. If you have these items, it would be best if you were prepared to have a fighting chance against whatever is thrown your way.

Adhesive Bandages

These are used for minor injuries such as a scratch or a small cut. The idea is to keep the wound clean and the dirt and bacteria out.

Bandages

Larger, non-adhesive bandages can be wrapped around a wound or injury to both covers and keep pressure on it. These bandages typically come in an elastic type of material.

Sterile Gauze Pads

When you have more extensive wounds or a wound bleeding quite a bit, sterile gauze is used to clean the wound and then keep pressure on it while still absorbing the blood.

Adhesive Tape

This tape can be used to hold bandages and gauze in place.

Antiseptic Wipes

These are very important to clean wounds with. Using an antiseptic wipe can lower the chances of infection.

Antiseptic Ointment

Once the wound is clean, using an antiseptic ointment before covering and bandaging a wound can help further reduce infection.

Disinfectant

This chemical can wash out wounds and injuries before any treatment. It can also sterilize tools like tweezers, thermometers, and scissors before use.

Tweezers

These items can help remove small items lodged in a person's skin or wound.

Scissors

These can be used to cut anything from bandages to clothing that's in the way. A pair of scissors is a must in any first aid kit.

Disposable Gloves

Gloves protect both the person receiving first aid and those giving it from infections and contaminating open wounds. Only work on somebody with gloves, especially if they have exposed wounds.

Pain Relievers

The pain relievers in a first aid kit are usually not very strong since they will all be over-the-counter medicines. Ensure you are careful before giving anyone a pain reliever because they may hurt the medication. Pain relievers should only be used as a last resort.

Thermometer

Out in the wilderness, fever and hypothermia are genuine possibilities. A thermometer can be a great help in detecting signs of conditions.

Blister Pads

When you constantly move around in the wild, you are more than likely to get blisters, especially when you start hiking, rock climbing, or other activities that require you to be more active than usual. These blister pads can relieve pain from blisters.

Instant Cold Packs

These are like ice packs, so their purpose is precisely the same. They can be used to reduce the pain and swelling of various injuries.

Hydrocortisone Cream

This cream can relieve pain and itchiness from insect bites and allergic reactions you might suffer from in the wild.

Antidiarrheal Medication

From touching a plant to drinking unfiltered water, there are many ways you can get diarrhea in the wild; having something to calm your stomach and combat the symptoms is always a good idea.

Antihistamines

Many things in the wild can cause allergic reactions, and depending on the severity of the allergic reaction, you probably won't have much time to react. Having antihistamines with you is always extremely important.

CPR Mask

These masks make CPR safer for both the person receiving it and the one giving it. You never know when something might go wrong and must give a stranger CPR.

Emergency Blanket

Although we've already covered the uses of an emergency blanket, it still has a place in your first aid kit and throughout the rest of your camping gear.

Eye Drops

So, eye drops are to clean or lubricate your eyes. In doing so, you can relieve the effects of minor irritations caused by various factors.

Safety Pins

Safety pins can be used in various ways, notably in fastening bandages or holding slings together.

Tourniquet

A tourniquet's primary purpose is to temporarily reduce blood flow to an area so that a wound can clot and, thus, the bleeding can stop.

First Aid Manual

A first aid manual can share information with an inexperienced person during an emergency. These manuals usually have instructions on dealing with various injuries and conditions.

WHAT TO DO IN EMERGENCIES

An emergency while camping is unavoidable. Something going wrong in life is entirely unavoidable. That is an unfortunate rule of life. The best we can do is prepare for when something goes wrong and know what to do in those situations. I can give you a list of possible emergencies and some advice on how to deal with them, but my advice is not medical advice and should be taken only as suggestions. Each situation is different, and each situation will require a different approach. A first aid course is the only natural way to prepare for every situation.

Possible Emergencies You Might Face

Bleeding

When someone gets cut and has a bleeding open wound, the first step is to clean the wound. However, depending on the severity, this might not be possible. Be sure not to make any wound worse when trying to treat it. If cleaning the wound might cause more damage, skip this step.

The next step would be to apply pressure directly on the wound. When you do this, wear gloves and ensure the bandage or gauze you use is clean and sterile.

While keeping pressure on the wound, elevate the wounded limb when possible. This will reduce blood flow to the area, allowing clotting and reducing blood loss.

Finally, seek professional medical attention immediately.

Fractures and Sprains

Something as simple as slipping on a rock can cause a fracture or sprain. So, being prepared for these types of emergencies is essential.

First, you will want to completely immobilize the injured area, which can be achieved through a splint. This will keep the area from being injured any further.

Applying a cold pack will be your next step, as it will reduce both pain and swelling. Adjust the splint as the swelling goes down to ensure no further injury.

Once again, after stabilizing the injury, immediately seek professional medical attention.

Burns

When you have open flames around you, it is probable that, at some point, somebody will get burned. When this happens, the first step is to get the source of the burn away from the person.

You will then want to cool the burned area by running cold water over it for at least ten minutes.

When the wound is cooled, use a clean dressing to cover it and seek professional medical attention immediately.

When treating burns, be very careful. This treatment is effective for first-degree burns, but more severe burns require immediate professional attention. It is also important not to apply any ointments or cream, as this will seal the heat inside the wound and cause more damage.

Heat-Related Illnesses

During the warm summer months, heat-related illnesses are a real possibility you will face at some point.

Your first step will be to move the affected person into a shaded and cool area. This stops their temperature from rising further.

Next, you will help them remove as much clothing as possible, incredibly any tight or constricting clothing they may have. This will help their body cool down.

Next, the person should drink cold water to start cooling their body from the inside. While doing that, place cold, wet clothes and ice packs on their bodies.

Lastly, you guessed it, seek professional medical help immediately. While doing this, keep the person conscious and ensure their body temperature decreases and their symptoms do not worsen.

Hypothermia

Just as heat-related illness is a reality you could face one day, so is hypothermia. This often occurs when someone gets wet in cold environments, but this is not exclusively required.

When someone suffers from hypothermia, you should immediately move them to a warm and dry area. Once there, remove any wet clothing they may have and replace it with dry layers, whether it is new clothing, blankets, or other dry layers that protect them from the cold. They should be wrapped up as warmly as possible.

If the person is awake, they should be given warm fluids to drink so that their body temperature can also increase from the inside.

Once again, the final step is to seek professional medical assistance immediately.

Allergic Reactions

There are a wide variety of allergens found in the wild, some of which we may not be aware that we are allergic to. An allergic reaction can threaten your life. People aware of any severe allergy should always carry an EpiPen.

For mild reactions, the antihistamine in your first aid kit should help combat these reactions. You should immediately seek professional medical assistance for anything more severe than a mild reaction.

One of the most important things to consider during an allergic reaction is staying with the person and monitoring them until help arrives. If you don't think help will arrive, take the person with you to where help can find you.

Getting Lost

When moving around in an unfamiliar environment, which can look pretty the same to the untrained eye, it is easy to wander off and get lost.

When this happens, your navigation equipment can help you determine where you are and where to get to. If you cannot do so, you should stay where you are and avoid getting lost any further while finding shelter as soon and close by as possible. It would be best if you also tried to signal for help by making noise, creating a fire, or finding another way to draw attention.

Dealing With Animals

Animals are often one of the major attractions of a destination, but they also come with risks. The best way to minimize the risk of a dangerous encounter with wild animals is by taking steps to keep them away from your campsite. This is, however, not guaranteed to work, and you will need to know how to deal with them as well.

Keeping Animals Away From Campsites

The primary item that will attract animals to your campsite is food. So, this is where we'll start. Storing your food properly will be the first step to keeping animals away from your camping. By keeping your food in airtight containers, we can keep the smell of food from attracting most animals.

It's also good to store your food where most animals cannot get to it. The best place to do this is ten feet above the ground and four feet from the trunk of a tree. A pulley system is excellent in this situation.

Since this is only sometimes possible, some national parks have set up bear boxes and lockers for your use. This will keep your food and scented items safe and away from any animal that might be attracted to them.

Be 100 yards away from your shelter and storage areas when preparing food. This will help keep animals away from your camp itself. When you are done preparing food and eating, properly wash all your dishes and utensils immediately. Leftover food and smells on your plates and utensils can attract animals to your camp.

Lastly, you will need to evaluate scented items. Before going on your adventure, find unscented alternatives for as many products as possible. For the items you cannot find unscented versions of, please keep them in airtight containers and store them with your food.

Dealing With Animals in National Parks

Coming across animals is inevitable. Then again, they are, in fact, part of the appeal. So, when you find animals in the wild, you will want to remain safe. The first tip is to stay 25 yards away from nonpredatory animals like deer and at least 100 yards from animals like bears. While keeping your distance, you should not be able to feed the wildlife. However, if you can feed animals, don't do it. You might not realize it, but feeding animals can cause the entire ecosystem to collapse.

While you are exploring, stick to designated hiking trails and campgrounds. Venturing into other areas could lead you directly into the habitat of some animals. This might not only prove dangerous to you but can also disturb the fragile balance of the wild.

Another great way to avoid getting too close to animals is to travel in groups and make constant noise. Animals are less likely to approach large groups and even less likely to approach a noise they don't know.

SO, WHAT DO WE KNOW?

By following these tips, you will be well-prepared for whatever emergency nature throws your way. Everything from a paper cut to encountering a dangerous animal in the wilderness should be a breeze.

Now, we must investigate what you will eat while you are away.

6

CAMPING COOKWARE AND MEALS

Your camping experience is almost completely sorted out. One of the last things we'll look at is the equipment we will use to make the fantastic food that will sustain us while adventuring. We've already covered food safety in the wild quite by now. So, we can focus on the essential tools and even some fun recipes.

COOKING GUIDELINES FOR NATIONAL PARK CAMPING

One of the significant impacts on our food in the wilderness is hygiene. Keeping our areas clean and hygienic can be extremely difficult with all the wild around us. This often leads to our food not being entirely sanitary and safe, which is why antidiarrheal medication is so necessary. But we can try and prevent that from being necessary.

The first step in ensuring your food is safe is thoroughly washing your hands before handling any food. We often find ourselves touching a tree for balance, grabbing a rock to pull ourselves up, or breaking our fall by extending our hands to the ground. This is all normal behavior, but we don't know what germs are crawling around on the surface of whatever we touch. Soap and water are necessary so that no microscopic pests enter our food and bodies.

The same goes for your cooking utensils and equipment. Before you use anything, clean it thoroughly, even if it is already clean. This helps ensure that contaminants that may have made their way onto your equipment are scrubbed away.

When you finally get to the cooking portion, use a camp stove or grill instead of an open fire. This further reduces the chances of contaminants making their way into your food. Of course, an open fire is a significant part of camping, so don't be discouraged from using it in small amounts. Just remember to prioritize safety.

When cooking meat out in the wilderness, you don't always have the luxury of controlling and monitoring the heat it receives as well as you could at home. This makes it extremely important that you take any steps to cook your meat properly. A food thermometer is a great addition to help you with this, but in a pinch, you can cut the meat open. Meat that is not adequately cooked can cause illness. So, you might also want to avoid meats such as fish, pork, and chicken when camping.

When washing your hands and equipment, ensure you do so at least 200 yards away from any water source. The same rule applies to dumping out any wastewater. Remember, we want to stay safe and preserve the park for future visitors.

Lastly, make sure you don't leave any food out. If you are not immediately consuming the food, ensure it is stored in an airtight, clean, temperature-appropriate crusher.

Storing and Preparing Food

As we've already covered by now, store your food in airtight containers and keep it out of reach of animals. I want to add an extra element: label all your food products. The labels should include the contents of the container, the date they were prepared, and the date they were stored. This will not only help with organization but also keep track of whether food is still safe to consume or not.

Another tip to keep food fresh for longer is to focus more on nonperishable foods, such as canned food, than fresh ingredients. In this way, the ingredients are kept in an airtight and safe container until the time you need them, and you can rest assured that your chances of having food that has gone bad are a lot less.

For the fresh ingredients you take with you, cut the ingredients up and pack them in pre-measured packets before leaving. This means you don't need to worry about having a clean surface to work on while out in the wild, and your cooking times are also decreased quite a lot.

Lastly, dispose of your food waste properly. Keeping your waste in airtight, sealable bags is the first step to ensuring safety. You will want to designate a specific area in your camp to keep your waste in and keep it in a lockable container. Ensure you frequently throw this trash away in a designated area and wash your lockable container each time. This will help to keep your campsite hygienic, animal-free, and smell-free.

COOKWARE

Now that we know how to stay healthy and clean while cooking in the wilderness, let's investigate the equipment and tools used for cooking.

#55—Camping Stoves

A camping stove can make your life a lot easier in the wild. You can use it for various things, such as boiling water for coffee, warming up your meal, or creating a delicious treat.

As with everything else, there are a few different options for you to choose from.

Canister Stoves

These compact little stoves usually have a canister containing a pressurized mixture of butane and propane attached to it. These stoves work great in moderate weather and allow you to control the flame precisely. This means your food is less likely to be burned, but you still enjoy a quick boil time. One of the most significant drawbacks of these stoves is that they usually only have one burner, meaning you either need a few or can only cook one thing at a time.

Liquid Fuel Stoves

These stoves use fuel bottles filled with liquids such as white gas, kerosene, or unleaded gasoline to create a flame that gives consistent heat and works in cold weather and at high altitudes. This means the stove is well-suited for a more extended trip, winter camping, or mountain climbing adventures. The main drawback is that these stoves need to be primed and maintained quite regularly.

Alcohol Stoves

Using either denatured alcohol or methanol as fuel, these stoves are incredibly lightweight and affordable. They are perfect for a quick backpacking adventure where you need more space. Their biggest drawback is that they produce less heat than other stove options, meaning they take longer to warm up and boil anything.

Solid Fuel Stoves

These stoves are preferred for emergencies or very short trips. They make use of fuel tables or hexamine blocks. This makes the stove simple and reliable, but as with the alcohol stoves, your biggest drawback is that they don't produce much heat. This increases your cooking time quite a bit.

Wood Burning Stoves

I would not suggest these stoves as the flame is an open fire. These stoves need to constantly be fed fuel, such as firewood, to keep going, and they don't align with the "leave no trace behind" philosophy of camping. However, they tend to be more environmentally friendly than other stoves.

Hybrid Stoves

These stoves allow you to switch between different fuel sources and are versatile. This adds to their flexibility in weather conditions where specific fuel sources may need to be revised. Their biggest drawback is that they often require specific attachments to be changed around, which can be complicated and impossible if one of the attachments goes missing or gets forgotten somewhere.

#56—Cooking Equipment

Now, we'll investigate the actual equipment to cook your food. These will be your pots and pans. They might seem like a nonissue, but choosing the correct pots and pans for your camping adventure can significantly impact your enjoyment.

Stainless Steel

We are all quite familiar with stainless steel, as it's almost a constant in our lives. Walking into your kitchen, you might find that most of your utensils and cookware are made of stainless steel. This is because stainless steel cookware tends to be more durable and resistant to scratches and dents than other types of cookware. They also usually come with a multilayer design that allows the heat from your chosen stove to distribute equally.

Stainless steel cookware is also easier to clean and can resist rust and corrosion much better. However, they tend to be heavy and are poor heat conductors, which can increase your cooking time.

Aluminum Cookware

These cookware options are much more lightweight than your stainless-steel options and less durable. They are often coated or anodized to increase their durability slightly, but they still don't hold up to stainless-steel cookware.

However, they outperform stainless-steel variants regarding heat conductivity and usually have a nonreactive coating that gives them nonstick qualities. The biggest drawback with aluminum is choosing a coated or anodized option, as the aluminum might react to acidic or alkaline foods. These options are usually a lot more affordable than other cookware options.

Titanium Cookware

This lightweight option is solid, conducts heat quite effectively, and is usually coated with a nonstick coating so food does not get stuck, making it easier to clean. Titanium is also corrosion-resistant.

So, what is the downside of titanium cookware? Aside from being much more expensive than other cookware options, titanium cookware is less durable than aluminum and stainless steel.

#57—Grills

While cooking on a stove is usually expected of us, nothing is better than eating something grilled in the wilderness. For our non-meat-eating readers, there are many recipes for grilling certain fruits and vegetables. Out in the wilderness, I recently enjoyed a delicious grilled potato marinated in a mouth-watering sweet barbecue sauce. For our meat lovers, a nice piece of steak grilled to perfection cannot be beaten. But before our yummy meals, let's look at the grill options.

When choosing a grill, there are a few factors to look out for:

- What type of food do you plan on grilling?
- What size grill will your camping setup allow?
- Does it need to be portable and easy to move around, or will your camp remain stationary once set up?
- Will you have easy access to the type of fuel this grill requires?
- How much cooking space will you require to make food for your group?

Charcoal Grills

These are personally my favorite grills. There is just something about the smoky flavor that tickles my taste buds. These grills typically use charcoal briquettes or lumps for fuel, allowing you to place the food directly above the heat. This makes the grill perfect for sharing your food. To top it all off, these grills tend to be affordable.

On the downside, getting used to cooking on these grills takes time, and temperature control is quite difficult. It would be best to wait for the charcoal to heat up before using them. Finally, when you are done using the grill, you are also faced with much ash to clean up, which makes adhering to the no-trace philosophy more difficult.

Propane Grills

These quick and convenient grills use propane gas to create a fire to grill on. This means they are easy to use and require minimal cleaning. In addition, the grill is ready immediately upon ignition, and the heat it provides is constant.

On the downside, these grills and propane tanks cost a pretty penny and are bulky and heavy.

Portable Gas Grills

These are propane grills in a smaller and more compact version. They have many of the same benefits as propane grills, and some models even offer interchangeable cooking surfaces.

The smaller propane tanks don't last very long, and the grill may not offer as much cooking space as other options.

Electric Grills

These grills use electricity as the primary heat source and usually have elements beneath the grilling surface. This makes them a lot safer and more accessible than other grill options.

On the downside, they will require some power source to work, which means that unless you have a battery or generator, these won't do you any good.

#58—Coolers

When you go camping, taking a fridge with you is not always possible; even if you do, a cooler will always be essential. Coolers come in a variety of different sizes and designs. Picking a cooler is a personal choice, although I recommend using a hard plastic cooler that can lock to ensure safety and not attract wild animals. We won't focus too much on the different options here; instead, we'll focus on the benefits of having a cooler with you.

- Coolers are great at preventing your food from spoiling as they are designed to keep everything inside at a low temperature.
- A cooler will allow you to keep ice longer to enjoy a nice cold drink on a hot summer day.
- Coolers are highly convenient as they are usually portable. So, you can fill it with ice and drinks and take it with you while enjoying nature.
- Lockable plastic coolers keep the smell and the animals and germs out. This makes your food safer for you to consume and store.
- The materials that a cooler is made of are often focused explicitly on outdoor use so that your cooler can endure nature with you.
- You always have a wide variety of size choices when it comes to coolers, from large chest-like coolers that can hold everything you need to smaller coolers that

can hold a few drinks or food items and can easily be carried around by hand.

- Coolers are designed to become wet and even hold some water as your ice and other products melt over time. This design also means that your cooler is easy to clean, with some even allowing you to remove the interior thoroughly.
- Lastly, coolers are great for organization. Aside from giving you somewhere specific to store food and drinks, many coolers also come with add-ons that allow you to organize the inside of the cooler.

#59—Water Filters

Our last essential in this incredible journey is our water filters. Unfortunately, water in parks and the wilderness is not always safe for consumption. To ensure you always have safe, drinkable water, take some water filters. When you don't have access to safe water, your life may very well be on the line, especially during an emergency. So, let's look at the water filter options available to you.

Pump Filters

These are filters with a hand pump attached to them. Using the hand pump, you force the water through the filter cartridge, effectively removing many contaminants, including bacteria and viruses. By forcing the water through, you can filter water faster than waiting for a filter to do it automatically.

On the downside, these filters tend to be bigger and heavier than most other water filters, and the continuous pumping can be exhausting. Although these filters are more durable than others, they require much maintenance and cleaning.

Gravity Filters

These filters typically have space to add unfiltered water and then use gravity to filter the water out over time. This is great since you can leave it to filter on its own and do other tasks, but it also means you must wait longer for the water to be filtered. These filters are also usually large and heavy and require maintenance and cleaning.

Squeeze Filters

These filters have a lightweight design that makes them ideal for adventures where you don't have much space. Much like the pump filters, they work when you force water through a filter, which means they are also relatively fast.

Unfortunately, they usually can't quickly filter large amounts of water and require occasional backflushing and maintenance.

Straw Filters

These are great designs since they allow you to drink water straight from an unfiltered source. They are also light and don't take up much space. This also means that they don't require maintenance.

On the downside, they are not ideal for sharing with a group of people, and you cannot store amounts of unfiltered water like you can with other filter options.

UV Sterilizers

These are the best at removing bacteria, viruses, and protozoa. They are also lightweight and portable, and unlike other filters, they do not leave a taste in the water. Unfortunately, these sterilizers require battery power to work. They also need clear water. Otherwise, they don't work well or remove sediment and chemicals from the water.

YUMMY MEALS DURING CAMPING

When camping, it's almost as if one hand is tied behind your back when cooking. This can make it challenging to decide what to cook, so here are a few ideas for great-tasting and fun meals you can make.

Campfire Nachos

These are delicious and usually prepared in a pan or skillet over an open fire, such as your campfire.

Ingredients:

- one bag of tortilla chips
- Shredded cheese to taste
- two diced tomatoes
- two sliced jalapenos
- 8 oz container of sour cream
- 8 oz container of guacamole
- 1 lb ground beef

Directions:

1. Cook the ground beef completely. It should be thoroughly cooked and ready to serve.
2. Layer the tortilla chips, tomato, and jalapenos in a pan or cast-iron skillet.
3. Add the ground beef on top of the layers.
4. Cover the ground beef with cheese.
5. Place the pan or skillet on your campfire until the cheese is melted correctly.
6. Serve with sour cream and guacamole.

One-Pot Pasta

A one-pot pasta meal may be perfect when you have limited cooking space on your camping stove. This recipe means you don't have to worry about some food getting cold while the rest is still cooking.

Ingredients:

- 16 oz box of pasta (macaroni works best)
- one diced tomato
- 2 cups tomato sauce
- one sliced onion
- ½ garlic clove
- Italian seasoning
- Salt
- Pepper
- 1 cup grated cheese (optional)

Directions:

1. In a large pot, sauté onion and garlic until fragrant.
2. Add tomato sauce and seasoning to the pot.
3. Bring the mixture to a boil.
4. Add pasta.
5. Cook until pasta is tender, occasionally stirring.
6. Serve with grated cheese.

Grilled Veggie Skewers

This is a great healthy and vegetarian-friendly option. It can be the centerpiece of your dinner or a mid-afternoon snack. Whenever you are enjoying it, it is quick and easy to make.

Ingredients:

- Assorted vegetables, such as bell peppers, mushrooms, cherry tomatoes, and onions, are sliced or cut into bite-size pieces.
- Olive oil
- Garlic powder
- Salt
- Pepper

Directions:

1. Thread the vegetables onto a skewer stick.
2. Brush the vegetables with olive oil and then sprinkle with spices.
3. Grill the skewers on an open campfire or your grill until the vegetables are tender and only slightly charred.

7

CAMPING ETIQUETTE, TIPS, AND HACKS

N ow that we have the essentials covered, it's time we looked into our behavior while camping and some tips and tricks that can make camping more manageable and more fun.

CAMPING ETIQUETTE

When it comes to camping, there is specific expected behavior. These are not strict rules for camping; they are just usual courtesies that all campers practice to ensure those around them enjoy their time in the wilderness equally.

- **Keep the campsite clean:** Make sure your waste and trash are neatly packed away so they won't attract animals or detract from the beauty of nature.

Dispose of your trash frequently in proper areas so the campsite does not stink or overflow.

- **Keep the noise down:** Most people are there to get a break from the city's hustle. This means spending quiet and relaxing evenings listening to the sounds of nature. Don't make much noise all night; be respectful during the day.

- **Be considerate of others:** Campsites usually don't mark boundaries too obviously as this might impose on the beauty of nature. This entails being mindful of imposing the privacy of others, even if there is a clear and short path to where you are going through the middle of someone else's camp.

- **Follow fire safety protocols:** Almost every campsite will have some flammable material with them. When a fire breaks out, everyone is at risk. So, be sure to follow safety protocols so that you do not endanger the lives of other campers.

- **Leave no trace:** We have referenced this philosophy several times. The basic idea behind this is to make as little impact on the park as possible. Do not move rocks around, pick flowers, break tree branches, or do anything else that might leave signs that humans have been there. In this way, you protect the beauty you see and preserve it for others to enjoy.

- **Be respectful of the animals:** Keep your distance from any animals you encounter, and do not feed them. If you interact with the animals, you might upset the fragile balance of the entire ecosystem. Animals may change their eating behavior, abandon habitats, or even abandon their youth if humans get too close.

- **Be friendly:** Be friendly and welcoming when you meet other campers and adventurers in a park. You don't need to invite them to your camp for dinner, but a simple hello goes a long way. Being friendly will often also get you tips about a rare event that might be happening or a beautiful spot to visit. It also makes the experience feel more welcoming and enjoyable to others.

CAMPING TIPS AND HACKS

To make camping life a bit easier, there are always tips and hacks to discover. I'll share a few with you here, but you can discover a lot more by searching online, joining camping forums, engaging with fellow campers, and experimenting.

- **Pool noodle tent stakes:** You can use a pool noodle cut to size and cut open lengthwise to cover your tent stakes. This makes them stand out in the darkness and protects your feet if you accidentally walk into one.

- **Water bottle lanterns:** If you fill a water bottle and then attach a headlamp to the bottle with the light facing it, the water will help spread the light around and create a beautiful makeshift lantern.
- **Homemade fire starters:** Using cotton balls and petroleum jelly, you can make a small ball that, when exposed to sparks or fire, will burn for a few minutes, and help start a fire. You must melt some petroleum jelly, dunk the cotton balls in the liquid jelly, squeeze out the excess jelly, and store your fire starters in an airtight container. Do this before going on your trip.
- **Water jug ice packs:** No matter how good your cooler is, any ice in it will melt over time. So, freeze your water jugs instead and use them as ice packs in your cooler to keep your other items cool. The plus side is that you get ice-cold drinking water as the ice melts.
- **Single-use soap:** A vegetable peeler slices a soap bar into single-use slivers. This allows you to minimize your soap and leave it in the wild.

My last camping trip hack for you is just a piece of advice. Don't expect anything from your camping trips. By creating expectations, you create the chance to be disappointed. Expect nothing each time and leave it up to the trip to surprise you with what it offers.

WAIT! BEFORE YOU GO...

You're ready and raring to go, but before you do, please take this opportunity to open the door to a lifetime of camping adventures for someone else.

Simply by sharing your honest opinion of this book and your own experience with camping, you'll show new readers where they can find all the knowledge they need to make a success of outdoor life.

JUST ONE CLICK!

Thank you so much for your support. Happy camping!

CONCLUSION

Camping is more than an experience—it is a lifestyle you must experience at least once. When you realize the joys a camping adventure can give you, you'll start planning your next trip before the one you are on is even finished.

You can take up this adventure alone when you need a break from life or take your family for a great bonding experience. You can even have an adventure with your friends. Regardless of how many people go with you, the memories you make while camping will last you a lifetime.

Of course, we've focused on camping in national parks since that is the safest, most convenient, and easily accessible option. However, you can adapt what you have learned from this guide to whatever adventure you choose, whether in a national park, in the wild, in your home country, or else-where. The possibilities are truly endless.

In this guide, we've looked at all the essentials to make your camping trip the best experience. You should now be able to plan your camping trip easily, having all your documentation ready and knowing exactly what to look for without hesitation.

We've covered everything you need to take with you to make your campsite not just a place to exist, but somewhere you can kick your feet up, take a deep breath, and truly enjoy the magic of nature around you.

You can now decide what tent, sleeping bag, sleeping pad, blanket, hammock, and chair best suits your needs. Your campsite becomes your mobile home once you have all these in place. This is where you will spend most of your time. Here, you will eat, sleep, and relax when you are not off having an adventure.

Of course, your camping site should appeal not only to you but to those you take with you as well. As we discussed, children, specifically teenagers, might be more difficult to introduce to camping. However, it is possible by working with them and allowing them to feel they have input into this adventure. Allowing them to help choose the adventures and what fun will be had while you are in the wild will encourage your children to enjoy camping again and again.

When you have children with you, the risks of camping do increase, regardless of what precautions you take. But when precautions are taken, you can ensure you are well-prepared when something goes wrong.

I could go on forever about this lifestyle, but finishing this book gives you everything you need to enjoy your camping adventures. Remember that each camping trip is an opportunity to learn, and there is always more learning for us to do out there. To help others learn the basics of camping, I would appreciate it if you left a review for this book wherever you got it or wherever you can review it. This helps other campers find the book and learn how to enjoy their adventure.

So, what are you waiting for? You've read everything there is to read, so put this book down and look at where your nearest camping site is! It is time for your adventure to begin.

GLOSSARY

- **Bear box:** A strong and secure container designed to store food and ensure that wild animals cannot reach it.
- **Camp chair:** A typically lightweight and collapsible seat that can easily be transported.
- **Camp shower:** A portable device that allows the user to create a makeshift shower almost anywhere.
- **Campfire:** An open fire that can be used for warmth, cooking, and light at campsites.
- **Campfire cooking:** Cooking your food on the campfire instead of using other equipment.
- **Campground:** An area designated for camping use, which can sometimes also allow the use of trailers, mobile homes, and RVs for a limited duration.

- **Camping cookware:** Normally durable and lightweight pots and pans for outdoor use.
- **Camping grill:** A portable grill that can use various fuel sources to allow cooking in remote areas.
- **Campsite:** A designated campground area where campers can set up equipment.
- **Canopy:** An overhang created with a tarp or large fabric that allows shade and protection from rain.
- **Carabiner:** A metal clip with a spring-loaded bar that acts as a gate. Usually used in climbing equipment.
- **Compass:** A navigation tool that uses Earth's magnetic field to point north.
- **Cooler:** An insulated storage container that regulates temperature and keeps the contents at a lower temperature for longer.
- **Firestarter:** A portable and compact device that quickly creates fire.
- **First aid kit:** A collection of basic supplies that can be used in various medical emergencies.
- **Headlamp:** A compact lamp designed to be worn on your head.
- **Lantern:** A light source that can be either hung or placed. These lights can be powered by batteries, solar, or consumable fuels.
- **Leave no trace:** A camping philosophy designed to ensure campers make as little impact on the

environment as possible. This philosophy ensures that campers leave nothing in nature that is not naturally found there and minimize the damage to nature from their stay.

- **National park:** A designated protected area that the government manages to preserve natural beauty and sites of cultural significance.
- **Sleeping bag:** An insulated bag designed to be slept in while providing warmth.
- **Tarp:** A waterproof sheet made of lightweight materials.
- **Trekking poles:** A stick-like piece of equipment designed to give the user extra stability when navigating the wilderness.
- **Water filter:** A device used to purify water and make it safe for human consumption.
- **Wilderness:** An undisturbed natural area.
- **Wildlife:** Animals that naturally inhabit the wilderness. This includes mammals, birds, insects, and reptiles.

REFERENCES

America the Beautiful - The national parks & federal recreational lands annual pass. (n.d.). USGS. Retrieved May 4, 2023, from https://store.usgs.gov/pass

Anderson, L. A. (Ed.). (n.d.). *Insect repellents: Safe and effective use.* Drugs. https://www.drugs.com/article/how-to-safely-use-insect-repellents.html

Andrea. (2019, March 2). *Spring camping: The ultimate list of tips, essentials, and destinations.* Embracing the Wind. https://embracingthewind.com/spring-camping-tips/

Anita. (n.d.). *Camping without a car: Transport, gear, food, and cooking.* Pitchup Outdoors. https://www.pitchup-outdoors.com/camping-without-a-car-transport-campsite-food-and-cooking/

Annual passes. (n.d.). NSW National Parks. https://www.nationalparks.nsw.gov.au/passes-and-fees/annual-passes

Backpacking cookware 101: Titanium, aluminum & stainless steel. (2022, December 15). The Summit Register; MSR. https://www.msrgear.com/blog/backpacking-cookware-materials-titanium-steel/

Backpacking stoves: How to choose the best. (2018, September 4). REI. https://www.rei.com/learn/expert-advice/backpacking-stove.html

Bahou, A. (n.d.). *Five ways to ward off a wild animal attack.* ABC News. https://abcnews.go.com/US/story?id=3307344&page=1

Batteries for camping. (n.d.). Reliable Batteries. https://reliablebatteries.net/blog/47-batteries-for-camping

Bergdoll, E. (2021, March 30). *What are the different types of tents?* Curated. https://www.curated.com/journal/6000/what-are-the-different-types-of-tents

Binwani, P. (2021, December 2). *50 best camping quotes & captions for nature seekers — The gone goat.* The Gone Goat. https://www.thegonegoat.com/inspiration-and-tips/camping-quotes-captions

Bittel, J. (2019, May 20). *How to stay safe around wild animals.* National Geographic. https://www.nationalgeographic.com/animals/article/safety-animals-wildlife-attacks-national-parks

Bor, K. (2020, October 19). *Fall camping tips: How to prepare and stay warm.* Bearfoot Theory. https://bearfoottheory.com/fall-camping-tips/

Burley, E. (2022, December 29). *Camping in spring? Here's how to do it right.* Gone Camping Again. https://gonecampingagain.com/camping-in-spring/

Cagle, S. (2023, March 17). *59 Easy camping foods that are tasty meals.* Brit + Co. https://www.brit.co/camping-food/

Camp Jelly Admin. (2017, February 16). *Start planning your spring camping trip with these tips.* Jellystone Park. https://www.campjellystone.com/start-plan ning-your-spring-camping-trip-with-these-tips/

Camping recipes. (n.d.). BBC Good Food. https://www.bbcgoodfood.com/recipes/collection/camping-recipes

Camping stove buying guide. (n.d.). Snow and Rock. https://www.snowan-drock.com/expert-advice-and-inspiration/buying-guides/camping-stove-buying-guide.html#:~:text=There%20are%20there%20in%20types

Chandler, T. (2023, February 21). *The benefits of investing in a quality camping cooler.* Gritroutdoors. https://blog.gritroutdoors.com/the-benefits-of-investing-in-a-quality-camping-cooler/

Choosing a backpacking water filter. (2018, September 4). REI. https://www.rei.com/learn/expert-advice/water-treatment-backcountry.html

Cindy. (n.d.). *Do you need an ax for camping?* Van Camping Life. https://vancampinglife.com/do-you-need-an-axe-for-camping/

Clines, J., & Clines, L. (2018, September 28). *No-car camping: Is it possible with kids?* Eco Family Travel. https://ecofamilytravel.co.uk/no-car-camping/

The complete guide to visiting national parks. (2022, July 6). KOA. https://koa.com/blog/the-complete-guide-to-visiting-national-parks-national-park-guide/

Cooking in camp. (2022, June 22). U. S. National Park Service. https://www.nps.gov/subjects/camping/cooking-in-camp.htm

The different types of stoves and their best uses. (2018). Big Sky Fishing. https://www.bigskyfishing.com/camping/camping-stoves-types/

Do you need a multi-tool for backpacking? (2021, April 15). Outdoor Is Home. https://outdoorishome.com/multi-tool-for-backpacking/

Eleven tips for planning your 2023 spring camping trip. (2023). Small Country

Campground. https://smallcountry.com/updates-%26-about-us/f/11-tips-for-planning-your-2023-spring-camping-trip

Eleven uses for trekking poles besides hiking. (n.d.). Cnoc Outdoors. https://cnocoutdoors.com/blogs/blog/11-uses-for-trekking-poles-besides-hiking

Elizabeth. (2019, August 22). *Genius camping ideas for your next trip.* The Dating Divas. https://www.thedatingdivas.com/101-genius-camping-ideas/

Escobar, L. (2017, February 15). *The five golden rules for visiting national parks.* Pura Aventura. https://pura-aventura.com/travel-stories/the-5-golden-rules-for-visiting-national-parks

Essential documents you need when visiting a U.S. national park. (2017, December 15). Visit USA Parks. https://visitusaparks.com/essential-documents-shouldnt-leave-home-going-u-s-national-park/

Everything you need to know about cooking on a camping trip. (2015, September). Good Living. https://www.environment.sa.gov.au/goodliving/posts/2015/09/happy-campers-part-two

Everything you need to know about fall camping. (2021, October 5). Fresh off the Grid. https://www.freshoffthegrid.com/fall-camping-tips/

Fall camping tips | What to pack for fall camping, meal ideas, and more. (2021, September 27). KOA. https://koa.com/blog/fall-camping-tips-what-to-pack-for-a-fall-camping-trip-more/

Felton, C. (2014, June 12). *Ten top tips to prepare your kids for camp.* Stuck on You. https://www.stuckonyou.com.au/blog/10-top-tips-prepare-kids-camp/

Fenton, L. (2022, January 24). *Nineteen tips for camping with kids.* Parents. https://www.parents.com/fun/activities/outdoor/19-tips-for-camping-with-kids/

Fifteen campground etiquette rules everyone should follow. (2019, September 20). WPLG. https://www.local10.com/travel/2019/09/20/15-campground-etiquette-rules-everyone-should-follow/#:~:text=Keep%20it%20clean.

Fifteen camping dinner ideas everyone will love. (2022, May 28). Fresh off the Grid. https://www.freshoffthegrid.com/camping-dinner-ideas/

Fifteen camping etiquette tips: How to be the camper everyone loves. (2017, May 15). Broken Head Holiday Park. https://www.brokenheadholidaypark.com.au/5577/15-camping-etiquette-tips-how-to-be-the-camper-everyone-loves/

Filson, M. (2023, May 2). *Forty-five easy camping recipes that go beyond burgers &* *s'mores.* Delicious. https://www.delish.com/cooking/menus/g27615055/ camping-food-cooking-recipes/

First-aid checklist. (n.d.). REI. https://www.rei.com/learn/expert-advice/first-aid-checklist.html

The five best camping grills for 2023. (2022, June 21). Beyond the Tent. https://www.beyondthetent.com/best-camping-grill/#:~:text=Grills%20in%20general%20run%20on

Five national park safety tips you need to know. (2023, March 27). InsureMyTrip. https://www.insuremytrip.com/travel-advice/travel-safety/national-park-safety-tips/

Five tips for choosing the best camping blanket. (2021, June 7). Denali Home Collection. https://denalihome.com/blogs/fandemonium/tips-for-choosing-the-best-camping-blanket

Five ways to prepare for summer camping. (n.d.). Recreation.gov. https://www. recreation.gov/articles/list/5-ways-to-prep-for-summer-camping/1698

Forty-five tips for foolproof fall camping. (n.d.). The Wilderness Society. https:// www.wilderness.org/articles/article/45-tips-foolproof-fall-camping

Four reasons camping is much more comfortable when you take a portable generator. (2022, April 17). Generator Place. https://www.generatorplace.com.au/4-reasons-why-camping-is-much-more-comfortable-when-you-take-a-portable-generator/#:~:text=With%20a%20generator%2C%20you%20can

Genius hacks to make camping with kids fun & stress-free. (2018, February 21). The Pragmatic Parent. https://www.thepragmaticparent.com/great-tips-camping-kids/

Greising-Murschel, J. (2020, July 2). *Twelve useful tips for camping in national* *parks.* Let's Travel Family. https://www.letstravelfamily.com/camping-in-national-parks/

Haenicke, S. (2022, October 20). *Ten things to know before camping in a US* *national park.* TheTravel. https://www.thetravel.com/things-to-know-before-camping-in-a-us-national-park/?newsletter_popup=1#the-perks-of-having-a-park-pass

Hiking and camping. Do you need a compass? (2021, April 8). GogglesNMore. https://www.gogglesnmore.com/blog/hiking-and-camping-do-you-really-need-a-compass/

Holmes, J. (n.d.). *Different types of sleeping bags for your camping adventures.* Cool of the Wild. https://coolofthewild.com/types-of-sleeping-bags/

Hostetter, K. (2011, February 10). *Sleeping bag buying guide.* Backpacker. https://www.backpacker.com/gear-item/sleeping-bag-buying-guide/?scope=anon

How to choose a sleeping pad. (n.d.). MEC. https://www.mec.ca/en/explore/about-sleeping-pads

How to choose and use trekking poles and hiking staff. (2023). REI. https://www.rei.com/learn/expert-advice/trekking-poles-hiking-staffs.html#:~:text=Trekking%20Poles%3A%20Sold%20as%20a

How to choose camping sleeping pads & camping mattresses. (n.d.). Evo. https://www.evo.com/guides/how-to-choose-a-sleeping-pad

How to choose cookware. (n.d.). REI. https://www.rei.com/learn/expert-advice/cookware.html

How to choose sleeping bags for camping. (2023). REI. https://www.rei.com/learn/expert-advice/sleeping-bag.html

How to choose the best camping blanket: 5 key factors to consider. (n.d.). BEARZ Outdoor. https://bearzoutdoor.com/journal/how-to-choose-the-best-camping-blanket-5-key-factors-to-consider/

Choose the best type of sleeping bag for camping in any season. (n.d.). KOA. https://koa.com/blog/how-to-choose-the-best-type-of-sleeping-bag-for-camping-in-any-season/#:~:text=Below%2C%20we

How to deal with emergencies while camping. (2015, April 17). Mapping Megan. https://www.mappingmegan.com/first-aid-tips-for-camping/

How to go no-car camping and caravanning. (n.d.). Pitchup. https://www.pitchup.com/guides/camping/camping-without-car/

How to introduce your kids to camping. (n.d.). KOA. https://koa.com/blog/how-to-introduce-your-kids-to-camping-family-camping-tips/

How to keep animals away from your campsite. (2017, March 13). GORE-TEX Brand. https://www.gore-tex.com/blog/how-to-keep-animals-away-from-campsite

How to prepare for emergencies while camping. (2022, May 6). Seven Corners. https://www.sevencorners.com/blog/travel-tips/how-to-prepare-for-camping-medical-emergencies

How to prepare kids for camp. (2022, May 5). Camp Tekoa. https://camptekoa.

org/blog/item/5-how-to-prepare-kids-for-camp

How to treat a first-degree, minor burn. (n.d.). American Academy of Dermatology Association. https://www.aad.org/public/everyday-care/injured-skin/burns/treat-minor-burns#:~:text=Immediately%20 immerse%20the%20run%20in

Huden, Z. (2022, September 27). *Seven tips for fall camping comfort.* Therm-a-Rest. https://www.thermarest.com/blog/7-tips-for-fall-camping/

Hussain, A. (2020, October 11). *The 10 Best Camping Hammocks.* Upgraded Points. https://upgradedpoints.com/travel/hiking-and-camping/bestcamping-hammocks/

The importance of having a first aid kit. (2018, February 1). Fox 40 International. https://www.fox40world.com/post/the-importance-of-having-a-firstaid-kit

Insect repellent guide: Deet vs. picaridin. (2019, July 9). REI. https://www.rei.com/learn/expert-advice/insect-repellents.html

Jacobs, C. (2023, January 14). *Twenty-three easy camping meals to make family trips a breeze.* The Spruce Eats. https://www.thespruceeats.com/easy-camping-recipes-5179202

James, J. (2019, August 14). *Survival matches or lighter.* Survival Freedom. https://survivalfreedom.com/survival-matches-or-lighter-whats-themost-reliable-in-the-wild/

Jerrard, M. (2016, June 8). *Dealing with emergencies while camping.* Waking up Wild. https://wakingupwild.com/dealing-with-emergencies-while-camping/

Johansen, A. (2022, November 21). *11 top uses for a camp ax.* Axe Adviser. https://axeadviser.com/what-is-a-camp-axe-used-for/

Kairis, A. (2017, June 7). *Camping safety: How to avoid wild animal encounters.* Blue Ridge Outdoors Magazine. https://www.blueridgeoutdoors.com/gooutside/camping-safety-avoid-wild-animal-encounters/

Krebs, J. (2022, March 3). *Tarp camping: Pros and cons of using a camping tarp.* Masterclass. https://www.masterclass.com/articles/tarp-camping

Laney, D. (2020, May 2). *Twelve reasons why you should invest in a camping cooler.* Refrigerator Planet. https://refrigeratorplanet.com/campingcooler-benefits/

Lasco, G. (2016, October 25). *Campsite etiquette: Eight tips for good camping manners.* Pinoy Mountaineer. http://www.pinoymountaineer.com/2016/ 10/campsite-etiquette-eight-tips-for-behaving-properly-on-camp.html

Levene, A. (2018, August 8). *A backpacker's guide to personal hygiene while camping.* Backpacker. https://www.backpacker.com/skills/beginner-skills/ prof-hike-a-backpacker-s-guide-to-smart-personal-hygiene/?scope=anon

Lewis, B. (2021, May 26). *The golden rules of camping etiquette.* OARS. https:// www.oars.com/blog/the-golden-rules-of-camping-etiquette/

Lightcap, J. (n.d.). *When backpacking, how much water should I carry?* Into the Backcountry. https://intothebackcountryguides.com/backpacking-skills/when-backpacking-how-much-water-should-i-carry#:~:text=A%20role%20of%20thumb%20that

Mandagie, E., & Mandagie, B. (2022, March 21). *Camping in the spring: 20 essential spring camping tips for a memorable weekend.* The Mandates. https:// www.themandagies.com/camping-in-the-spring/

Martin, B., & Bento, M. (2020, October 8). *How to choose a backpacking sleeping pad.* GearLab. https://www.outdoorgearlab.com/topics/camping-and-hiking/best-sleeping-pad/buying-advice

Matthews, B. (2017, March 9). *A quick guide to rope & cordage for camping.* OnDECK; DINGA Online. https://ondeckby.dinga.com.au/quick-guide-rope-cordage-camping/

Michelle. (2017, April 27). *The basics of battery power for camping.* Ben & Michelle. https://benandmichelle.com/the-basics-of-battery-power-for-camping#:~:text=In%20a%20nutshell%20it

Morgan, P. (2020, August 21). *Ten tips for camping with kids and babies.* AFAR Media. https://www.afar.com/magazine/10-sanity-saving-tips-for-camping-with-young-kids

Murphy, P. (2014, August 18). *Ten knife types: Outdoor blades.* GearJunkie. https://gearjunkie.com/camping/knife-types-common-outdoors-blades

Navigation. (2010, September 21). The Hiking Life. https://www.thehikinglife. com/hiking-and-backpacking-skills/navigation/

Nine tips for spring camping | Planning your early spring camping trip. (2023, February 16). KOA. https://koa.com/blog/tips-for-early-season-camping/

Nineteen camping hacks and tips that will improve any camping trip. (2019). KOA. https://koa.com/blog/camping-hacks/

Paran, S. R. (2019, December 31). *Five of the best camping pillows.* Wander Era. https://wanderera.com/camping-pillows/

Peggy. (2021, April 18). *Why you should use fire starters when camping.* Noah's March. https://www.noahsmarchfoundation.org/why-you-should-use-fire-starters-when-camping/

Peter. (n.d.). *How to keep animals (and bugs) away from your campsite: Science supported.* Decide Outside. https://decideoutside.com/how-to-keep-animals-away-from-your-tent/

Pilson, G. (2020, October 12). *Fifteen campsite lighting ideas to illuminate your night.* Outdoria. https://outforia.com/15-campsite-lighting-ideas-to-illuminate-your-night/

Practical tips for camping in a national park. (2023, January 13). Southerner Says. https://southernersays.com/2023/01/13/camping-in-a-national-park/

Reasons why you might need a camping cooler. (n.d.). SkiPeak. https://www.skipeak.net/blog/reasons-why-you-might-need-a-camping-cooler

Rules and regulations. (n.d.). U.S. National Park Service. https://www.nps.gov/places/rules-and-regulations.htm

Sachs, A. (2022, June 22). *How travelers can stay safe during encounters with wild animals.* Washington Post. https://www.washingtonpost.com/travel/2022/06/22/safety-wild-animals-travel-vacation/

Schatz, T. (2022, August 11). *The complete and most awesome guide to fall camping.* Backroad Ramblers. https://backroadramblers.com/the-best-fall-camping-tips/

Seven different types of camp stoves. (2022, April 4). Trek Baron. https://trekbaron.com/types-of-camp-stoves/

Seven different types of lights for camping. (2018, April 24). Nearly Wild Camping. https://nearlywildcamping.org/7-different-types-of-lights-for-camping/

Seven ways to safely watch wildlife. (n.d.). U. S. National Park Service. Retrieved May 14, 2023, from https://www.nps.gov/subjects/watchingwildlife/7ways.htm

Shane, & Chetna. (2021, February 15). *Five practical ways to use a carabiner while camping [hacks & tips].* Meandering Spirits. https://meanderingspirits.com/blog/travel/5-practical-ways-to-use-a-carabiner-while-camping/

Six important knots you should know. (2019, May 6). Copake Camping Resort. https://copakecampingresort.com/6-important-knots-you-should-know/

Sleeping pads: How to choose. (2019, July 9). REI. https://www.rei.com/learn/expert-advice/sleeping-pads.html

Sleeping pads – Types and features. (2019, December 27). Camotrek. https://camotrek.com/blogs/news/sleeping-pads/

Sleeping pad guide. (n.d.). Backpackers. https://backpackers.com/outdoor-guides/sleeping-pad-guide/

Spridgen, D. (2023). *How to choose a camp chair.* REI. https://www.rei.com/learn/expert-advice/how-to-choose-a-camp-chair.html

Sweet, D. (2019, November 25). *Checklist for a camping first aid kit.* TripSavvy. https://www.tripsavvy.com/first-aid-checklist-for-camping-498450

Switchback Travel Staff. (2023, March 17). *Best backpacking sleeping pads of 2023.* Switchback Travel. https://www.switchbacktravel.com/best-backpacking-sleeping-pads

Ten ways that duct tape can help you at the campsite. (2021, February 20). West Country Parks. https://www.westcountryparks.co.uk/10-ways-duct-tape-can-help-you-on-the-campsite

Thornton, E. (2016, June 15). *The best and worst ropes to use while camping.* Idaho State Journal. https://www.idahostatejournal.com/outdoors/xtreme/the-best-and-worst-ropes-to-use-while-camping/article_55fa4e36-6aad-5f81-92e2-8ac6190a0ea2.html

Tips for camping with kids. (n.d.). REI. https://www.rei.com/learn/expert-advice/camping-kids.html

Tips for planning your fall camping trip. (2019, September 19). GO-KOT. https://campingcot.com/blogs/news/tips-for-planning-your-fall-camping-trip

Twenty-five of the most useful camping tips and hacks for 2021. (2021, July 25). The Planet D: Adventure Travel Blog. https://theplanetd.com/camping-tips/

Twenty-five types of tents for camping, backpacking & hiking. (2022, April 13). Urban Dare. https://www.urbandare.com/types-of-tents/

Twenty-seven easy camping meals to make camp cooking a breeze. (2020, March 17). Fresh off the Grid. https://www.freshoffthegrid.com/27-easy-camping-meals/

Two types of camping shovels | Buyer's guide for selecting the best camp shovel for your needs. (2022, April 9). Trek Baron. https://trekbaron.com/types-of-camping-shovels/

The ultimate guide to sleeping bags. (n.d.). Go Outdoors. https://www.goout doors.co.uk/expert-advice/sleeping-bag-guide

Van Der Post, G. (2022, May 17). *Why should you use leisure batteries for camping trips?* Gone Travelling. https://gonetravelling.co.uk/why-should-you-use-leisure-batteries-for-camping-trips%EF%BF%BC/

Vukovic, D. (2019, April 16). *How to go camping and get into nature without a car.* Mom Goes Camping. https://momgoescamping.com/camping-without-car/#:~:text=If%20you%20are%20camping%20without

Vukovic, D. (2020, November 27). *The ten types of camping tents.* Mom Goes Camping. https://momgoescamping.com/types-camping-tents-with-photos/

Wang, P. (2013, June 5). *Forty-one camping hacks that are borderline genius.* BuzzFeed. https://www.buzzfeed.com/peggy/camping-hacks-that-are-borderline-genius

Watson, R. (n.d.). *Tips for safely visiting national parks.* National Park Foundation. https://www.nationalparks.org/connect/blog/tips-safely-visiting-national-parks

Welch, S. (2021, June 8). *How to plan a summer camping trip.* Farm and Dairy. https://www.farmanddairy.com/top-stories/how-to-plan-a-summer-camping-trip/667866.html

What is the best kind of blanket for camping? (2021, February 24). Ocean Outdoors. https://oceasoutdoors.com/blogs/adventure-awaits/best-camping-blankets

What to wear when camping. (2022, February 15). KOA. https://koa.com/blog/what-to-wear-when-camping-camping-clothes/

Wildeck, T. (2020, January 25). *What is a carabiner, and what can I do with one?* The Dyrt Magazine. https://thedyrt.com/magazine/gear/what-is-a-carabiner/

Wright, R. (2020, November 23). *Advantages of using fire starters on camping trips.* Working Mom Blog; Outside the Box Mom. https://outsidethebox mom.com/advantages-of-using-fire-starters-on-camping-trips/

Your fall camping checklist (n.d.). The Wilderness Society. https://www.wilderness.org/articles/article/your-fall-camping-checklist

Zauberman, K. (2023, April 13). *Get ready to cook over an open fire with these fun camping recipes.* The Pioneer Woman. https://www.thepioneerwoman.com/food-cooking/meals-menus/g40012064/camping-recipes/

www.ingramcontent.com/pod-product-compliance
Lightning Source LLC
Chambersburg PA
CBHW060227030426
42335CB00014B/1365